You're Not The Person I Hired!

A CEO's Survival Guide To Hiring Top Talent

By
Janet Boydell,
Barry Deutsch,
Brad Remillard

authorHOUSE™

1663 Liberty Drive, Suite 200
Bloomington, Indiana 47403
(800) 839-8640
www.AuthorHouse.com

First published by AuthorHouse 4/18/2006

ISBN: 1-4208-8170-1 (sc)
ISBN: 1-4208-8169-8 (dj)

Library of Congress Control Number: 2005907907

Printed in the United States of America
Bloomington, Indiana

This book is printed on acid-free paper.

Contents

Acknowledgments

We originally anticipated completing this book in three months. The project actually took more than a year. The result, even though we sometimes felt as if our lives and business were on hold, has been well worth the effort.

The three of us, through our preparation and research over the last year in writing this book, have gained a greater understanding of what really happens when companies hire executives.

We've commissioned original research, undertaken surveys, spent countless hours in coffee shops with CEOs debating the finer points of hiring top talent, and invested untold hours among ourselves in midnight conference calls working through the chapters of this book (we *did* still have to earn a living during a few of the daylight hours). Our workshops, consulting projects, and executive search practice have taken a quantum leap forward in value as we've been able to share the results of this massive year-long project.

In reality, we've been preparing to write this book for the last 15 years as we've taught and executed the concepts daily, primarily through our executive search practice. We've amassed an amazing store of knowledge from interacting with 20,000 CEOs and key executives, tens of thousands of interviews, and well over a thousand search assignments.

The body of knowledge and insights we share in this book are very much a part of the people whom we've had the pleasure to know. The three of us do what we do because, deep down, we enjoy making a difference—a difference in the careers of very talented candidates, and a difference in the successes of the executives who hire them.

For all of us, perhaps there were numerous paths over the past few decades we could have taken that might have provided an easier road to success. But none of them would have been as rewarding.

With deep appreciation and gratitude for those rewarding experiences, we would like to thank the following people for their contributions:

- Our clients, for having the confidence in us to continually help them hire Top 5% Talent. A large portion of our success comes from repeat business for the same clients. Although we recognize that they keep bringing us back because of the results we obtain, we'd also like to think they enjoy working with us in the hiring process as much as we do with them.

- Our candidates (a fair number of whom have become clients after having seen the effectiveness of their interviews), who have provided valuable insights and recommendations on how companies can be better at attracting top candidates.

- Trusted advisors who consult, coach, and advise their CEO clients and stay involved in the hiring process. These are the people who trust us enough to refer their most treasured and sacred clients. A few of these whom we would like to give special mention include Dana and Ellen Borowka, Mindy Kaplan, and Kathy Tricoli.

- The Executive Advisory Board of the American Association of Senior Executives (AASE), who have provided strong business advice and kept us on track in moving toward our vision of creating a business around the Success Factor Methodology.

- Henry DeVries and Denise Van Slyke at the New Client Marketing Institute, who are at the forefront of their profession in helping firms more effectively demonstrate their value. Henry and Denise were our editors in writing this book, and it could not have been done without them.

- Valuable insights regarding the hiring and recruiting process have come from working relationships over the years with Lou Adler, Jack Higgins, Mark Rutherford, Randy Gorrell, Mark Lorimer, Marilyn Momeny, and Gina Harpur.

- We're indebted to our staff, including our research and administrative team of Jennifer, John, Karen, and Patty. Your commitment and hard work continues to impress us every day.

- The Executive Committee (TEC), a worldwide organization of over 10,000 CEOs and key executives. We would particularly like to thank Richard Carr, President of TEC, and Rafael Pastor, Chairman and CEO of TEC. We need to thank all the folks in the Speaker Department of TEC who send us flying around the country to talk with CEO groups about the Success Factor Methodology™. We cannot express our appreciation enough to the members of TEC for the invitation to peek inside their companies to better understand the hiring process.

- A key element of the TEC organization is the Chairs, who facilitate small groups of CEOs around the country. We would like to thank the many Chairs who have invited us to speak before their groups. We would be remiss without specifically thanking our own personal Chairs: Steve Elson, Les Whitney, and Kevin Rafferty.

Finally, we've saved the best for last. We are deeply indebted to our families who have supported us far beyond the call of duty as the three of us made this journey over the past year. You've been there as we've made the painful sacrifices like basketball coaching we've missed, woodworking projects lying dormant in the garage, and family obligations for which we've sent others in our place. We could not have done it without your incredible support. We love you and thank you for it.

- Our wives, Martha Deutsch and Bev Remillard
- Our children, Marissa and Ben Deutsch, Courtney Raney and Burke Boydell, and Danna and Mark Remillard
- We would also like to dedicate a special remembrance to Scott Boydell, for his love and encouragement.

Introduction

The Top Ten Hiring Mistakes And How To Avoid Them

We wrote this book with one goal in mind: to help companies avoid hiring mistakes.

You're Not The Person I Hired! is a guide that can make sure the person you bring into a critical job is, in fact, the person he or she appears to be. Too often the managerial and executive hiring process is a case of mutually crossed fingers—both parties *hope* the match is a good one, and *hope* the gamble they're taking will pay off.

And then, regrettably, when Monday morning rolls around and the work begins, it all unravels.

Whose fault is it when the person who seemed like a fired-up go-getter turns out to be indifferent to goals she didn't set herself? Whose fault is it when the person hired to overhaul the organizational IT system turns out to be short-tempered, impractical, and a lousy communicator who alienates every functional department head? Whose fault is it when the new sales manager seems to have no impact whatsoever on penetrating two new markets—a mission-critical goal that he seemed fully capable of doing in interviews? *Whose fault is it when the person who shows up for the job isn't the person you thought you hired?*

We believe the blame lies squarely with the hiring process itself, and we have compiled evidence to prove it.

Our research focusing on more than 20,000 hiring executives during the past fifteen years has identified the most common mistakes made in hiring. Through the course of our analysis, we determined the actual failure rate for newly hired managers and executives reaches a staggering 56% in many mid-sized and large organizations. We wanted to understand why. Prior to writing this book, we analyzed the hiring practices of 225 executive hires in 134 target companies.

What we discovered was that almost every organization makes the same mistakes, over and over again. Most often, several mistakes occurred in each case. In nearly every situation, when new executives and managers failed to meet expectations, a major causal factor was that expectations had not been clearly defined in the first place.

Everything else fell out from there.

The ten most frequent mistakes, in reverse rank order, were:

10. *Desperation Hiring:* In 55% of searches, the hiring organization failed to budget enough time for the search, resulting in shallow sourcing and superficial interviews that failed to identify potential pitfalls.

9. *Ignoring Top Candidate's Needs:* 55% of searches were handled with a primary focus on the organization's needs and failed to build a compelling case for why top candidates should make the move.

8. *Failure To Probe For Core Success Factors:* The five best predictors of long-term success are self-motivation, leadership, comparable past performance, job-specific problem solving, and adaptability. A majority of searches failed to probe for these (56%).

7. *Fishing in shallow waters:* The search attracted only "Aggressive" candidates without seeking "Selective" and "Sleeper" candidates (62%).

6. *Performance Bias:* Interviews and offers were rewarded to the "best actor," not the best candidate (63%).

5. *Historical Bias:* The hiring company used only past performance to predict future results (68%).

4. *Snap Judgment:* Hiring teams relied too heavily on first impressions to make final hiring decisions (72%).

3. *Inappropriate "Prerequisites" Used Too Early In Selection Process:* Hiring teams placed too much emphasis on specific education, technical skills, and industry experience to screen out qualified candidates (76%).

2. *Superficial interviewing:* Candidates' backgrounds and claims were not deeply probed or verified (92%).

1. *Inadequate job descriptions* drove the hiring process; these focused solely on experience and skills, not company expectations. A staggering 93% of searches that resulted in new executive failure made this mistake at the outset.

The Causes Of Hiring Mistakes

In our experience, hiring mistakes are not caused by willful ignorance or negligence. Most often, new executive failure has several interrelated causes.

Inadequate preparation. Rarely had the hiring companies outlined a detailed, measurable definition of "success" that could be used to source, evaluate, and select candidates. Instead, they relied on outdated or insufficient job specs, focused around desired attributes, educational attainment, and so on.

Lack of information. After our work with the surveyed companies, nearly all dramatically improved hiring practices and (most importantly) the performance of new hires. We conclude, therefore, that at least one cause of their earlier hiring failures was not endemic organizational dysfunction, but a lack of information and training about how to hire more effectively at the executive level.

"Human nature." Interpersonal situations like interviews, conducted in a vacuum, are often guided primarily by gut feelings. Hiring team members who have not been trained to minimize these distractions are easily influenced by preconscious perceptions and nonverbal cues. When provided with a tool set designed to counterbalance these biases, interview team performance is far more likely to overcome distractions and focus on more critical success-based matters.

With the most common hiring mistakes and their causes in mind, we have developed and refined the Success Factor Methodology™. This structured approach to executive hiring helps our client companies avoid repeating predictable, avoidable hiring pitfalls that plague many high-level hires. We believe *every* organization—large or small, for-profit or nonprofit, public or private—is capable of using this methodology to significantly improve its hiring success at the executive and managerial level. This book will show you the way.

But it isn't easy.

There is only one way we've discovered to make sure your next executive or managerial hire is successful: Tightly define what success will look like before the search begins, and focus like a laser beam on verifying that each candidate you see has the demonstrated potential to create that success. The Success Factor Methodology requires a rethinking of almost every part of your hiring process. The progress you make will correlate directly with the amount of dedication, focus, leadership, and effort you expend. It works when *you* work—and there are no shortcuts.

We use the following eight steps to help companies hire Top Talent. You can use them too. When you've finished this book, you will have the tools you need to develop and implement a hiring methodology for your company.

The Success Factor Methodology

Step 1. Build The Success Factor Snapshot™

This tool drives all of the hiring practices. We work with our clients to develop this unique document, which ties an individual's performance to the company's operating plan and helps ensure that the CEO and other senior managers achieve their respective goals.

The Success Factor Snapshot clearly defines what the new executive must achieve during the first twelve to eighteen months, and dramatically increases hiring accuracy.

Step 2. Plan Collaborative Sourcing Strategy

Based on the Success Factor Snapshot, we work with the hiring team to develop a compelling marketing statement that will appeal to and attract Top 5% Talent. In addition, we brainstorm with the team to identify the best formal and informal networks to tap. The end result is a thorough sourcing plan that identifies specific channels where highly desirable Selective and Sleeper candidates may be reached. This ensures a deep pool of Top 5% Talent.

Step 3. Identify And Verify Success Prospects

When Top Talent are presented with a compelling opportunity, they are more willing to participate. Our approach is based on our ability to ensure that potential candidates grasp the company vision; we generate enthusiasm and energize candidates who would normally exclude themselves. In addition, through extensive phone and face-to-face interviews, we verify their ability to deliver results that were specified in the Success Factor Snapshot.

Step 4. Create Candidate Profiles

The strongest candidates' qualifications, assessments, resumes, and documentation are standardized and summarized, along with our Eight-Dimension Success Matrix™ form. This process calls attention to each candidate's unique value, highlights his or her strengths, and identifies any potential sticking points that will need to be overcome to ensure a successful hire.

Step 5. Coordinate Success Factor Interviews

This step helps separate the best *performers* from the best *interviewers*. The Success Factor Snapshot guides the development of interview questions and homework assignments; it uncovers the true success potential of each candidate. The Five Key Questions interview helps to determine not only who can do the job, but also who will be the most adaptable and fit into the company's culture and working environment. Once our client has identified the final one or two candidates, we conduct deep reference and background checks.

Step 6. Overcome Obstacles To Hire

Once a company and candidate have decided there is a potential match, there should be no surprises left to break the deal unexpectedly. Our approach identifies and helps overcome obstacles to completing the deal early in the process. We work through potential problems like relocation issues, family objections, counteroffers, and "cold feet."

Step 7. Facilitate Compensation And Benefits Negotiation

Savvy recruiting includes managing the process so that it doesn't fall apart at the eleventh hour. The time and money invested in a search project can be jeopardized in the final stages, so we don't wait until the client is ready to make an offer before bringing compensation issues to the table. When last-minute issues surface, as they inevitably do, we act as an intermediary, diplomatically ensuring that the search is completed to everyone's satisfaction.

Step 8. Transition and Follow-up

Once the deal is inked and the candidate has come aboard, we're still working to ensure a reasonable and smooth transition for the new executive. We facilitate assimilation coaching to ensure the new executive is successful from the first day.

We wish you success in your hiring Top Talent, and we hope the advice, tools, methods, and processes you are about to learn will help you to transform your business. We are always happy to hear from our readers and answer questions about the concepts in this book. Drop us a note at authors@impacthiringsolutions.com. We'd love to hear from you.

SECTION 1: YOU BET YOUR COMPANY

Chapter 1: Past Experience Is No Guarantee Of Future Results

> It's like déjà vu all over again.
>
> *Yogi Berra*

"Déjà Vu All Over Again": A Case Of Repeated Executive Failure

A couple of years ago, we worked with a $40 million Information Technology service company. The organization provided around-the-clock support services for large networks, telecommunications systems, and in-house IT systems.

At our first meeting with the CEO, he confessed, "We've experienced high growth over the past few years and predict we'll sustain at least double digit growth for the next five years. We're under-performing when it comes to bringing good people into the organization. It's frustrating. We know we need good leaders at the executive and senior manager level to take us where we want to go. We just can't seem to find them…and we keep making the same hiring mistakes over and over."

Growth plans depended on extending and expanding contracts for existing services to current clients, as well as gaining sizeable new clients. The firm wanted to become a sole provider for its clients' IT installation, support, and repair needs.

Unfortunately, the company not only had difficulty finding the right person for a critical position—the Vice President of Sales—but had also made recent bad hires in the position. In fact, of the last five executive-level hires, three had been replaced and one was on probation. Their upcoming search looked like a case of "déjà vu all over again."

The prior sales VPs did not deliver acceptable sales results. They had not brought in new contracts, opened new customers with new products, expanded existing contracts, or built the business. The CEO was increasingly frustrated because these previous VPs had come from larger companies that had grown rapidly. The CEO assumed this meant they were a perfect fit for his job. After all, they had "been there, done that."

Unfortunately, they failed.

They failed for a number of reasons.

- The client company's growth issues were significantly different than the challenges they had overcome in previous positions.
- Their past accomplishments were irrelevant—or at least not transferable—to the new position.
- They could not adapt to new situations.
- They were not able to produce the required results, and the hiring process had failed to reveal this fact.

While the company's lack of a strong VP of Sales was creating an immediate problem, it also contributed to a succession-planning dilemma. The company's "bench strength" was weak. When critical employees left, went out on leave, or even just took a few weeks' vacation, there was nobody waiting in the wings to fill in.

It was a precarious situation.

When we conducted an audit of the company's hiring practices based on the Success Factor Methodology, we discovered problems we have seen at many companies their size—and even larger.

- Hiring was the only process in the company that had not changed or been updated since the company started more than ten years ago.
- Hiring was the only process in the entire company that was not performed according to a documented process or methodology.
- They were using outdated sourcing, screening, and interviewing techniques that required no training or expertise.

- There was no uniform, specific process to assess candidates and evaluate them against each other.
- There was no marketing plan to attract good candidates.
- The company concentrated mainly on applicants who applied after seeing an advertisement.
- There was no accountability for bad hires (or good ones, for that matter).
- They had no process for establishing goals for an open position *before* they hired the candidate.

For their next (and hopefully last, at least for a long time) VP of Sales search, the CEO needed a methodology and process to help him determine how a candidate's past achievements and accomplishments directly related to the results he expected. And he needed a quantifiable way to rate candidates, both "in a vacuum" and against each other.

Prior to starting the search for a new Vice President of Sales, we conducted a Success Factor Methodology Workshop for the company's senior leadership team. As a direct result, the company revamped their hiring process using many of the techniques and tools you will find in this book.

The results were exceptional. The VP of Sales we helped the company locate and hire was still in the job three years later, and according to the CEO, the overall quality of new hires at every level is now much better.

The 56% Problem

The failure rate our client experienced with the VP of Sales position was painful for them, but it is not unusual.

When companies hire a six-figure executive, they expect them to "hit the ground running" and produce results quickly. But according to our surveys of more than 20,000 hiring executives over the past fifteen years and a review of published literature on the subject of executive failure, roughly *56% of newly hired executives fail within two years of starting new jobs.*

Frankly, 56% is worse than a flip of a coin.

Published studies and decades of direct experience bear out the findings. We have interviewed more than 10,000 hiring executives during the past two decades, and we suspect that the *actual* rate of executive failure and turnover in the first two years is even higher.

It goes without saying that a 56% failure rate is abysmal.

If a similar failure rate happened on the manufacturing floor, the plant would be shut down. If a company's financial statements were only accurate 56% of the time, it would be disastrous. And yet, year after year, organizations experience this syndrome and act as though they are helpless to overcome it.

Is the problem that these companies are not interviewing enough people? Or asking the right questions? Could it be that it is impossible to predict whether somebody can succeed in an open position before that person comes aboard?

No, no, and no.

Based on extensive research and experience, we have determined the most common root causes of much executive failure are:

- Focusing on irrelevant past experience and skills
- Nebulous expectations
- Failure to clearly communicate expectations up front
- Flawed hiring processes

The crux of the problem is that every company says it wants to hire a "Superstar" who will "succeed," but if you ask what a superstar looks like, or what "success" means in concrete terms like dollars, cents, percentages, time, headcount, and other hard numbers, you generally get a blank stare by way of reply.

Is it any wonder that new hires fail to meet expectations when those expectations are not clearly spelled out?

Picture This

You are the CEO of a $95 million company. You've just invested roughly $80,000 in search fees alone for a nationwide search to find a new Vice President of Operations.

The person you've hired looks like that much-vaunted "Superstar." She graduated from a stellar school, has more than fifteen years of experience, comes from the same industry, has great references, and breezed through all interviews with flying colors. The CEO and the hiring team are thoroughly impressed and have high expectations. They make her a generous offer. She accepts.

Now, see yourself twelve months down the road. The company's operations have not improved. In fact, they've fallen apart. The superstar's experience emphasized analysis and more analysis. Although she had great-looking credentials, her ability to execute and implement change was lacking. Production breakdowns have run rampant. Deliveries to customers have faltered. Quality has not improved. Costs have not been contained.

You decide to take action and terminate your "Superstar" for poor performance.

What happened? What went wrong? And, most importantly, are you going to learn from your mistakes?

Despite the time and tens of thousands of dollars invested in hiring high-level executives (not to mention multiples of salary that are lost indirectly through a bad hire), failure rates remain incredibly high. And hiring a search firm is no guarantee of success.

Every search firm promises they can find "Top Talent" or the "best of the best." (They have to promise this, or you wouldn't retain them.) But usually, that isn't good enough to ensure success. The problem is that most executive search firms focus on a candidate's past work history, or industry experience, or degrees, or titles, but *not* what is expected of the candidate in the future.

The Corporate Leadership Council, an association of human resource executives, reports that half of all new hires who quit prematurely complain about unclear expectations. *Executives fail to meet expectations because success was never clearly defined in advance.*

During the past twenty years, CEOs and boards of directors have often asked why half of the six-figure executives they hire don't measure up. We answer with questions of our own: "Measure up to what? What was the standard you were measuring against? What were the original measurable expectations you set when you first hired the executive? What defines quantifiable success, projected out for the next twelve to eighteen months?"

Direct And Indirect Costs Of Failure: The "Trickle-Down" Effects Of A Bad Hire

Business guru Peter Drucker has said, "Of all the decisions an executive makes, none are as important as the decision about people because they ultimately determine the performance capacity of the organization." Warren Bennis, professor of business at the University of Southern California and author of *Managing the Dream*, calls the search for Top Talent "the most significant problem facing all organizations."

According to a study by the Corporate Leadership Council, hiring the wrong executive can cost an organization as much as three times their annual salary. The Gallup Organization has noted that the cost of poor hiring decisions may even be much higher than previously estimated. Some researchers have calculated the cost of a bad hire can be as high as twenty four times the position's base salary.

Presidents, CEOs, Boards of Directors, and hiring managers should never underestimate the ramifications of a bad hire. The fallout can affect an entire organization, doing far more damage than leaving the position empty would have.

Think of all the lost opportunities and hidden costs associated with a bad hire. The total financial impact can include reduced time to market, lost revenue from incomplete projects, and failed execution of strategies. This results in untold lost profits and productivity.

While reasonable experts may disagree about specific salary-to-cost ratios, the fact remains that the cost of new executive failure is much higher than merely search costs and salary. Those are just two of the direct costs.

Indirect costs typically add up to much more.

Some of the direct and indirect costs noted in various studies we reviewed include:

- wasted salary, benefits, and severance
- lost recruitment fees and training costs
- lower personal productivity among dissatisfied employees
- disruptions caused by dissatisfied employees
- higher turnover rates among productive employees
- damages to reputation and market share
- lost management time
- increased stress and anxiety from people problems

Multiplied across ten million businesses in North America, it is obvious that bad hires cost billions of dollars every year. Sadly, this is a game in which everyone loses.

The person hurt most just might be the executive who was set up for failure. This person accepted a position based on a vague job description, and then found reality did not match up to their perceptions.

In 1997, a groundbreaking study by McKinsey & Company exposed the "war for talent" as a critical driver of corporate performance. Updated in the year 2000 and based on surveys of 13,000 executives at more than 120 companies and case studies of twenty-seven leading companies, the McKinsey team found that companies that do a better job of attracting and retaining Top Talent boost their performance dramatically. In fact, the top quintile (one-fifth) in the study earned, on average, twenty-two percentage points higher return to shareholders than their industry peers.

But what of the rest? The companies that scored in the bottom 20% in the McKinsey study earned no more for their shareholders than their peers. In other words, they got average to mediocre results.

The Cost Of One Bad Hire: A Worksheet

To help you get a more concrete idea of the costs of a bad hire, we've assembled the following worksheet. You should take the take the time to fill it out as completely as you can. Even if you guesstimate at times, you'll find the bottom line enlightening—and probably alarming.

Direct Costs

Hiring Costs	*Calculate for entire search, all candidates*	
	Recruiting fees	$
	Assessment/background check fees	$
	Employee referral incentives/fees	$
	HR department time and expenses	$
	Executive/department Interviewer time and expenses	$
	Travel expenses (candidates, families, HR, recruiters)	$
	Total Hiring Costs	$
Compensation	*Calculate for duration of employment*	
	Salary	$
	Bonuses	$
	Benefits	$
	Relocation costs	$
	"Perks" (autos, club memberships, etc.)	$
	Paid time off/vacation/sick pay	$
	Stock options	$
	Total Compensation Costs	$
Severance	Severance pay	$
	Legal costs	$
	Outplacement or retraining costs	$
	HR and other staff time/expenses related to termination	$
	Total Severance Costs	$
	Total Direct Costs	$

Indirect Costs		
Support Costs	Support personnel time and expenses (i.e., executive assistants)	$
	Office space, equipment, network resources, training	$
	Expenses, mileage, travel costs	$
Cost of Poor Performance	Poor execution (failed product launches, missed earnings targets, poor reputation due to missed on-time-deliveries/quality, etc.)	$
	Missed opportunities (losing business to competitors, being second in product launches, missed opportunities to enter new markets, etc.)	$
	Lawsuits (include legal representation costs, judgments, executive and board time, and expenses)	$
Cost of Poor Subordinate / Department Morale	"Trickle-down" cost of poor performance among subordinates, departments, and divisions (estimate if necessary)	$
	Turnover among subordinates due to poor morale, mismanagement (include costs of hiring replacements)	$
	Total Indirect Costs	$
	Grand Total: Direct and Indirect Costs	$

Our clients—even the ones who spend most of their days plotting profit-and-loss strategies in the executive boardroom—are often astounded when they see, in black and white, how much it really costs to hire the wrong person.

This book is designed to give you a structured set of tools and processes that will let you do for yourself what we do for our clients: identify and remedy the most common mistakes in executive hiring, and revamp your company's hiring process to be able to attract the Top 5% of Talent in your industry.

Who Are The Top 5%?

Top 5% Talent are the people you want working in your organization at all levels. While building an entire workforce of Top 5% Talent won't happen overnight, you've got to start somewhere, and it should begin in the executive ranks.

In the executive suite, the Top 5% are those rare people who outperform their peers and consistently create profitable businesses that grow at a sustainable rate.

Depending on the business and the industry, Top 5% Talent won't all look alike. But they all have one thing in common: Their performance outshines 95% of people in similar roles because they have a track record of delivering superior results. They don't settle. No matter how they do it, they make great things happen.

What you need is a reliable way to find and hire these people. But all too often, we've seen companies settle for hiring the "best" candidate from a pool of mediocre candidates. Instead of aiming for the Top 5%, they settled on somebody from the bottom third.

Why? Usually because those people are easier to find, cheaper to hire, and willing to fill a job that's been open "too long."

To those with that mindset, we ask: which surgeon would you turn to for open-heart surgery? The one who's easy to find, cheaper, and available to do your procedure earlier than anybody else? Or the one whose patients have a much better chance of surviving the surgery and thriving afterwards?

Let's suppose you're having initial consultations with heart surgeons. What kinds of questions would you ask? Would you be concerned about knowing where they went to school, what their grade-point averages were, where they did their rotations, how many years of experience they have as heart surgeons, or how many heart surgeries they have performed? (If so, you would be conducting a typical hiring interview with them.)

OR, are there more important considerations? How about the *results* of their previous surgeries? How was success for heart surgery determined for different patients? What percentage of their former patients now lead active lives, and for how many years after surgery do they survive? How did the heart surgeons adapt their experience and knowledge to unknown or new situations? What did the surgeons *learn from each patient?*

The second set of questions yields far more predictive information than the first. "Years of experience and number of surgeries performed" may sound good. But what if, during all those years of experience, one surgeon had a much lower success rate than others?

This example demonstrates precisely why focusing on candidates' *past experience* alone is the wrong way to approach hiring. There are far more critical facts that must be uncovered and evaluated—namely, their performance, results, success, and potential adaptability to your organization.

Why Do New Executives Fail?

Let's face it. No executive wants to fail. They don't fail because they are not smart enough; in fact, as a group, executives are some of the most brilliant people around. They don't fail because they aren't motivated; their drive and ambition are evident. And they don't fail because of unforeseeable events, lack of leadership ability, dishonesty, or a shortage of resources.

They fail because the traditional hiring process focuses on things (like schools, degrees, years of experience, past employers, etc.) that are not directly relevant, recent, or applicable to the hiring company's requirements and conditions.

Most executive searches eventually locate and place people who are "successful" in life. They've gone to the right schools. They've worked at the right places. They've earned impressive titles. In short, they look like winners.

But are they the best person for this job at this time? That depends on whether you know what you want.

Unfortunately, many companies buy into the idea that a superstar new hire will help the company to define success when he or she arrives. This is a monumental miscalculation. It's like starting to play high-stakes poker without knowing the rules—a very expensive way to learn. Setting clearly defined and quantifiable performance goals *before* the executive job search begins takes extra effort. (The Success Factor Snapshot is one of the best ways to get this done; see Chapter 5.)

Hiring executives are often so consumed with their daily functional roles—marketing, finance, strategy, or operations, for example—they might be tempted to skip setting clear expectations for new hires until after the candidate starts work. This is the fatal flaw. Successful candidates—those who beat the 56% rule—are recruited and screened based on specific expectations regarding future success.

Identifying what results the new hire should produce, along with clear expectations, performance management systems and rewards that accurately reflect those targets is a tricky process. There are no shortcuts. Defining what success will look like, *up front*, takes extra effort for the company, the hiring executive, and the search firm. But the payoff is worth the time, effort, and every dollar.

Executives who precisely match what is expected are significantly more successful at helping companies reach profit goals. In fact, client companies who have used the Success Factor Methodology have a 98% success rate when they follow our proprietary process. Because we offer a 100% satisfaction guarantee, we bet our company on the accuracy of our hiring methodology.

The Definition Of Insanity

One of Benjamin Franklin's most famous quotes is, "Insanity is doing the same thing over and over and expecting different results."

If the six-figure executives you hire were meeting expectations, you wouldn't be reading this book. You are one of the rare individuals who recognize the need to do something differently. You are not insane.

If you want to beat the hiring odds and overcome the 56% problem in your company, *there is a way*. If you have the will, the determination, and the "stick-to-it-iveness" to change what you have been doing to get better results, you will be guaranteeing that your next executive hire (and even *non-executive* hires) won't be Yogi Berra's "déjà vu all over again."

Unlearn Everything You Thought You Knew

To achieve better results, you need a better approach to hiring. But for many people, there's a sizable obstacle to hiring the Top 5%. That obstacle is a career-long accumulation of "a little knowledge" about hiring. Almost every client we have ever worked with had first to be broken of bad hiring habits before they could adopt new, productive ones.

One of the dirty little secrets of management is that when you're promoted, nobody ever tells you precisely *how* to manage, let alone how to be an outstanding interviewer. Most people are promoted on the basis of great achievements and talents in a specialized field (sales, engineering, logistics, whatever). Upon arriving in the managerial or executive suite, they're thrust into situations where they are expected to possess (or quickly develop) a whole new set of "soft" management skills, including putting the right people in the right job.

Hiring really good people isn't magic. It is a highly developed skill. Like other skills, it can be learned. But sometimes before you are able to learn a new skill, you must *unlearn* others.

Take typing, for instance. *Anybody* seated in front of a keyboard can create a basic document. Even if they've never been taught how to type, they'll manage to hunt-and-peck their way to a more-or-less decent-looking letter or memo. But it will cost an untrained person a great deal of time and frustration than somebody who's been taught proper touch-typing technique.

Add more training and skills in advanced word-processing, and a good touch-typist can whip out a letter that looks like it was professionally typeset. Meanwhile, the hunt-and-pecker is still struggling with "Dear John Smith, it has come to our attention..."

Unfortunately for life-long hunt-and-peckers, *the hardest person to teach touch-typing is the person who's been hunt-and-pecking for years.* That's because they've picked up, internalized, and reinforced so many bad habits for so long, they're highly resistant to change. It takes drastic measures to break those habits.

Some typing instructors use devices that block the typist's view of the keys; there's almost no other way to get those eyes *off* the keys. That's the habit they need to unlearn before they can improve.

Learning to hire well, believe it or not, is a lot like learning to touch type. If you've only hunted-and-pecked in your hiring for fifteen years, it's going to be very uncomfortable to change. Because you're going to have to *let go of* many of the things you've always believed, thought, and done in the past.

- Typical job advertisements (they're boring—throw them out)
- Traditional job descriptions (keep them in the personnel file where they belong)
- Tired "standard" interview questions (most of them are overused and useless)
- The "carousel" interview technique (stop sending candidates around and around the office to be asked the same basic questions over and over again)
- Preconceived notions about minimum education and years of experience (these factors *may* matter—then again, they may not)

In other words, before you can improve your hiring results, you've got to break your organization of its old hunt-and-peck ways. You and your hiring executives are going to have to unlearn everything you all thought you knew about hiring.

One Big Secret

For those of you who are "skip to the end" kinds of readers, we won't make you wait any longer. The One Big Secret to hiring Top 5% Talent is this:

You must design and put into place a hiring system that:

- precisely identifies what quantifiable results you want from your new hire during the first year,
- mines deep for the best candidates, no matter where they are,
- structures interviews to unearth the most relevant predictors of success,
- assesses accurately and moves only highly qualified candidates to the next step, and
- results in offers only to candidates who are capable of meeting your clearly defined expectations—the Top 5%.

Sounds obvious and probably sounds like what you're already doing, right?

But not really.

Everyone wants to hire better. Nobody wants to hire an average or mediocre candidate. Why, then, does everyone keep using the same ineffective hiring methods week after week, hoping for a better outcome?

The Success Factor Methodology helps companies avoid Ben Franklin's definition of insanity. This book will provide you with the road map to consistently hire Top 5% Talent.

Chapter Summary

❖ When newly hired executives fail to meet expectations, it's generally because **success was never clearly defined in advance.**

❖ To successfully hire a Top 5% candidate, companies need to **identify what results they want** from the new hire during the first year.

❖ Once there's a roadmap in place, **every other step of the hiring process needs to support** finding, interviewing, and closing the candidate who clearly demonstrates his or her ability to meet expectations.

Chapter 2: The Crapshoot Hiring Syndrome

> Informed decision-making comes from a long
> tradition of guessing and then blaming others for
> inadequate results.
>
> *Scott Adams*

Ask just about any executive or manager with hiring responsibility to
describe their hiring process. (No, really. Ask!)

Chances are, you'll hear something like this.

> "HR *manages our process. We advertise. HR screens the resumes that*
> *come in. I review the ones that make the cut. I pick the top contenders—*
> *the ones I want to talk to. HR calls them and sets up interviews. We*
> *bring them in, and the management team and I take turns conducting*
> *round-robin interviews. We narrow down our choices and prioritize*
> *our top two or three choices. We call them back for a final round of*
> *interviews. We huddle and pick the one everyone likes the best. Someone*
> *calls references. Then we make an offer and negotiate compensation with*
> *our first choice. If it doesn't work out, we either move on to the second*
> *choice or start the process all over again."*

Sound familiar? Sounds reasonable, doesn't it? Who *wouldn't* describe
their hiring process that way? Isn't that how everybody does it?

Well, yes and no. While it *is* a common process, not everybody uses
such a system. Those who have learned the hard way know **the
traditional hiring process is not a reliable way to hire the best
candidate.**

A useful process is reliable, in that it produces the same results over
and over again. A valid process organizes every action. It supports the
outcome. It manages all the details and orders them in a foolproof,
fail-safe sequence. A reliable process is independent of individuals and
produces predictable results.

A valid process makes a McDonald's sandwich taste the same whether it was purchased in Los Angeles, Tokyo, or Paris.

On the other hand, a pseudo-process is a related series of scattershot activities, not unlike the roll of a dice. Like the "hiring process" summarized above, a pseudo-process gives the appearance of systemization while it actually hinges on hope and luck.

The traditional hiring pseudo-process is based on the idiosyncrasies of each individual executive or manager. Like all pseudo-processes, it leads to random results. The only thing predictable about such a hiring process is that it's just about **guaranteed** to lead to the 56% problem.

We call this *The Crapshoot Hiring Syndrome*. It's an epidemic with several symptoms: dependence on luck, the illusion of clarity, tribal hiring practices, desperation hiring, and hiring based on "experience" and "skills" rather than success.

Dependence On Luck

So, why is Crapshoot Hiring not a reliable and valid hiring process? Because it depends on luck.

- **Luck in sourcing.** What are the odds that the Top 5% of available talent for your job opening can be reached through an ad, even if you could afford to publish the right ad literally everywhere? What are the odds they will read that ad in the brief period of time it is running?
- **Luck in timing.** What are the odds that the Top 5% just happen to be looking for a new position at precisely the same time you are seeking to hire a person?
- **Luck in screening.** What are the odds that HR will recognize the potential Top 5% candidate during resume screening? What are the odds they'll *miss* a good candidate because they're looking for the wrong things? The members of your HR team are the gatekeepers and the key holders; are you absolutely sure they know what you and your organization need?

- **Luck in interviewing.** What are the odds that the interviewing executives will effectively and legally probe to ensure a candidate can deliver the results you expect? Build and lead teams? Be able to adapt to your challenges? Successfully fit in with your culture?
- **Luck in evaluating.** What are the odds that everybody involved in the hiring process will be able to agree on the qualities of a Top 5% candidate—or what's critical, what's important, what's nice to have, and what's nonessential? What are the odds that the typical canned (often irrelevant) interview questions will reveal that information? Will you miss the best candidate for all the wrong reasons? Worse yet, will you lose a Top 5% candidate because of your poor hiring practices?
- **Luck in creating a compelling offer.** What are the odds that the Top 5% candidate can be wooed to join—and stay with—your company long enough to make the kind of impact you need them to make? What are the odds that geography, compensation, benefits, lifestyle concerns, or other obstacles that crop up at the last minute won't kill the hire?

A reliable and valid hiring system can move all of those things out of the realm of luck and into the realm of reality. The entire organization must learn and develop reliable, replicable processes to attract, hire, and retain the best of the best.

The Illusion Of Clarity

Part of the reason that companies end up suffering from the Crapshoot Hiring Syndrome is that they begin the hiring process by defining the kind of person they are looking for instead of the position they are trying to fill. For example: they want somebody with "good interpersonal skills." Or great "management skills." They want a "go-getter." A "leader." Somebody who's "results-oriented."

Exactly what do those terms mean? It's anybody's guess. Ask twenty people what "good interpersonal skills" are, and you'll get twenty different answers. Common hiring catchphrases are useless.

Even if you *could* get twenty people to define the catchphrases, how would you then know if they are the *right* new executive who will succeed in *your* company and culture?

The *illusion of clarity* dooms many failed executive and managerial hires.

It's not unusual to hear a President or CEO describe the person they think they're looking for in great detail. But the details turn out to be bullet points from the biography of the last person who held the job—the hiring team is "in the Clone Zone."

"We loved Jane. She's been very productive for us. So the next person should have an MBA from the Ivy League and 15 years of related experience in a Fortune 500 manufacturing firm. That's what Jane's background was, and I figure if we can find somebody else just like her, we're set."

They are simply trying to recruit a Jane Clone. But nobody else on earth is Jane. Six to twelve months later, the firm will probably be searching again, clueless about what went wrong (*"But she seemed just like Jane!"*), having wasted up to twenty-four times the Jane Clone's salary.

On the flip side, maybe the previous position holder was widely disliked or made a hash of things. In those cases, the hiring team can get stuck in the *Anti*-Clone Zone, listing all the things they disliked about the predecessor and looking for the exact opposite.

Either way, the resulting search is a *subconscious reaction to one person*, not a conscious and informed search.

"Tribal" Hiring Practices

"That's the way we've always done it."

How many times have we heard that phrase? Too many. The hiring process in most companies is simply based on the transference of "tribal knowledge." The methods used to define positions, find candidates, and interview candidates are based primarily on what the previous generation did, with no regard for whether they are actually reliable, effective, or predictive.

There are probably thousands of things in every organization that happen merely because "that's the way it's always been done here." Poor hiring practices are no exception to this rule. We speak with executives every day whose approach to hiring seems to be torn straight out of the "that's the way it was done when I was hired" playbook.

One executive in a consumer products food company made it a point to ask the same question of every single applicant for a key position in the Finance department. The question was, "What recommendations would you make to improve a firm's position in the telecommunications industry from being the number seven competitor to the number two competitor?" The question was arcane, complicated, and *utterly unrelated* to the open finance and accounting position. He may as well have been asking, "What was the ultimate impact of the coin-operated lint-picking machine on the rise and fall of the Byzantine empire?"

When we asked him *why* he was taking time out of each interview to ask the question, he looked us straight in the eyes and said, "Because that was the most difficult question I was asked back when *I* started at this company."

Sound familiar?

How many hiring practices in your organization are simply tribal rituals that have been perpetuated through the years?

Desperation Hiring

Desperation hiring, plain and simple, is making do with whoever shows up.

When there's a vacancy to be filled, many companies move into a "Panic Hiring" mode. After all, there's an empty desk. Work is piling up on it. Productivity and profits are at stake. It seems better to have somebody—*anybody*—in that chair than nobody at all.

When you're in Panic Hiring Mode, you want to fill the job *fast*, pressure becomes so intense, and compromises end up ruling the day. A two-week advertising stint is followed by two to three weeks plowing through hundreds of resumes, leading to interviews with a small gaggle of applicants. Usually, but not always, they're the *wrong candidates*.

The majority of "panic hiring" candidates are usually people who are out of work and eager to get back to a regular paycheck. They aren't being any more selective about their next job than the company interviewing them. These candidates need a job *fast*. So even if their foot doesn't precisely fit into your company's glass slipper, they'll chop off a toe to make it fit.

What these applicants lack (or have too much of) in terms of experience and past responsibilities, they make up for in eagerness, enthusiasm, and "can-do" spirit.

"Leap buildings in a single bound? Can do"!

"The company's verging on bankruptcy and the last guy in this job ran away to Australia with the coffee money? I can't wait to come on board!"

"Board meetings are run by the same rules as American Gladiator*? Sounds like the kind of culture that really clicks with me!"*

When one of these applicants gets hired and then fails, whose fault is it, really?

It's not entirely theirs. They did what any desperate job hunter would do—they told hiring authorities exactly what they wanted to hear. They may even have sincerely believed that they were capable of doing the job, even if it was a bit of a stretch for them.

The fault really lies with outdated sourcing, interviewing, assessing, and selection techniques that perpetuate poor hiring accuracy.

A search at the executive or managerial level deserves the patience and selectivity that will deliver the *right* candidate—not just a candidate that's "good enough."

Hiring Based On "Experience" And "Skills" Rather Than Success

Interviewer: *What a great resume! You seem to have had a lot of interesting experience. Could you tell me more about yourself?*

Candidate: *Absolutely. I was born a coal miner's daughter...*

What does "experience" really mean?

A twenty-year veteran manager who's been a marginal performer still has twenty years of experience. Like the heart surgeon who has lost 76% of patients over the course of 24 years, you can't tell just from a number of years whether experience has produced good or bad *results*.

Experience, knowledge, and skills are not proven predictors of success for *your* job opportunity. It's past *results* that count—and how they help predict whether a candidate is able to succeed in *your* open job.

Too many hiring executives through the ages have been dazzled by the surface brilliance of a candidate's background. Too few have managed to come up with a systematic way to probe that background deeply and match up past experience with future deliverable results. The core problem is confusing "experience" with the *ability to do the job*.

25

These are just a few of symptoms of Crapshoot Hiring that we have helped our clients overcome. We will draw your attention to other flawed hiring practices as we move through the rest of this book.

Taking The Crapshoot Out Of Hiring: A Case Study

One of our clients—a company that manufactures ethnic food products—wanted to change fundamentally the way they went to market. For three decades, they had always focused on sales, but the new CEO realized that if they were going to grow and capture more of the market, they would need to shift from a sales orientation to a marketing-driven strategy.

The company was a solidly run family-owned business with very traditional values. The average employee tenure was 20 to 30 years—employees came, stayed, and retired. It was a good place to work, and there was definitely a comfortable routine in place. The new marketing strategy would need to be driven and implemented by a new marketing executive.

Due to the culture of the firm, the impact of the planned strategic change had the potential to unleash chaos, confusing and upsetting long-time employees who were quite happy with "business as usual."

After four months of interviewing typical marketing professionals who had no demonstrated ability to manage a quantum shift in a tight-knit company, the firm decided it was time to try something new.

When we first met with the executive management team, we immediately hit them with hard questions.

- Had anyone on the senior management team actually shifted an entire organization from sales-driven to marketing-driven? (They hadn't.)
- How would they interview, assess, and measure the candidates' abilities and past accomplishments at guiding a major shift like

the one they planned? (They had no idea, just a job specification.)

- Did their current organization chart accurately reflect the new direction they wanted the company to take? (It didn't.)
- Did their interviewing accurately clarify specific expectations, and include appropriate adaptability issues? (It didn't.)
- Had they considered searching outside the ethnic parameters of their consumer products? (No, they didn't think it possible.)
- Did they have concrete assessment and measuring tools in place to help them measure the key objectives or candidates against one another and recognize the best fit when they found it? (They didn't.)

This was a tough search assignment for a number of reasons, but we knew we could help them.

Before beginning the actual search, we conducted one of our in-house Success Factor Workshops for the entire hiring team. These workshops help everyone understand how to attract and hire a Top 5% candidate. We then guided our client based on the workshop concepts by implementing our Eight-Step Success Factor Methodology on the search project.

The end result was well worth the effort. Our client found the kind of leader they wanted. The Success Factor Methodology yielded an executive who had successfully ushered not one, but two companies through the challenge of moving from a sales orientation to a marketing orientation, in comparable organizations.

The new hire had worked outside the U.S. in at least nine other countries, with great exposure to different cultures, and had successfully dealt with sensitive organizational transitions in the past. These were all measurable accomplishments that were directly related to the needs of this job opportunity.

In the end, the company's new hire and strategic shift were both successful.

If you want to learn how to do the same in your organization, keep reading. The following chapters will give you all the tools you need to make your next search a properly managed, reliable and valid hiring process versus a systemic crapshoot.

Chapter Summary

❖ **Typical hiring practices aren't a reliable or valid process—they're a crapshoot.** You bet your company, roll the dice, and hope you'll get what you need.

❖ **Typical hiring practices are a pseudo-process that rely on luck, not fail-safe procedures.** A structured, systematic process develops only when you identify and unlearn old bad habits and then practice new ways to achieve desired results.

❖ **Recruiting ads and interviews shouldn't focus on what the last person in the job had;** instead, they need to focus like a laser beam on what the next person will need to *do*.

❖ **The most pervasive symptoms of Crapshoot Hiring are:**
  ➢ Dependence on luck
  ➢ The illusion of clarity
  ➢ Tribal hiring practices
  ➢ Desperation hiring
  ➢ Hiring based on "experience" and "skills" rather than success

❖ Success in hiring comes from having a **structured, systematic, rigorous business process** focused on attracting and assessing Top 5% Talent.

Chapter 3: Maybe If We Give It More Time, It Will Work Out

> Great leaders are approachable people with a low tolerance for poor performance.
>
> *Dan Wertenberg, TEC Chair and Speaker*

Whether you are the newly appointed CEO or you started the firm in your garage twenty-seven years ago, the first step to staffing up with Top 5% Talent is to remove deadwood.

Culling the herd is astonishingly simple in theory, but maddeningly difficult in practice. Especially when an executive knows intuitively that somebody should really be moving along, but can't quite force himself to "make them available to industry."

We have seen reluctance to force change many times through the course of our work. The names and places change, but the story is always the same. A top-level manager has been badly placed—perhaps promoted beyond capabilities (a victim of the "Peter Principle"), or hired without a set of concrete expectations to guide him. The manager is now causing problems that almost everyone in the company can plainly see. Despite all the available evidence, leadership is reluctant to cut the manager loose quickly and find somebody else who is able to succeed.

Instead, the hiring manager delays, hoping against hope that the new hire just needs a little longer to "get it" and start to produce results.

This is a colossal miscalculation.

When expectations are not being met, it is almost guaranteed that performance will not improve with more time. In most cases, more time will just make things worse.

The "Ostrich Approach"

For eons, people have maligned the ostrich for its stupid reaction to dangerous situations. Legend has it the largest bird on Earth stands still and "sticks its head in the sand" when it senses danger approaching, believing that a threat not seen is a threat vanquished.

We laugh at the ostrich. We know better. We know that problems continue to exist, even if you choose not to look at them.

But while the tale of the "head-in-the-sand" ostrich is widespread, it is also not true. So maybe we aren't as smart as we thought.

In point of fact, when an ostrich feels threatened, it does *not* bury its head in sand. Like most species that have survived into modern times, the ostrich's first response to danger is to *run*. Only if the ostrich cannot run will it turn to Plan B and attempt to become invisible. In those cases, the bird lies down as flat as it can on the ground, with its head and neck straight out, to minimize its profile as much as possible. (Apparently this strategy actually works to deter predators.)

So, it turns out for all these years, people—mostly business writers—have been giving the ostrich a bum rap. The critter is not quite as stupid as we have been led to believe.

All of which is a long way of saying, whether or not it's literally true, the "ostrich approach" is still a lousy approach to problem-solving.

You know that you cannot fix a problem by burying your head in the sand—or, more accurately, by lying low—and hoping that danger will simply go away. With that in mind, if a new hire (or longtime employee, for that matter) is not living up to expectations, you must be emotionally strong enough to recognize the problem and take immediate action to remedy the situation.

A 1999 *Fortune* magazine cover story on executive failure drove this point home with a brutally honest insight from Larry Bossidy, former CEO of AlliedSignal: "If you have three or four people in the mill and some run short along the way, you can't wait. You've got to make a change right then."

The title character in Kenny Rogers' 1970s hit "The Gambler" doled out some free advice just before he moved on to that great card table in the sky. It applies equally well to cards, life, and management practices.

"Know When To Hold 'Em, Know When To Fold 'Em, Know When To Walk Away, Know When To Run…"

A bad hire or promotion is usually evident within the first three to six months. Three to six months—not three to six quarters, and definitely not three to six years. Between 1995 and 2001, the rates of executive turnover soared by 53% (according to a study conducted by Booz Allen Hamilton). Obviously, cutting the deadwood in top positions is becoming increasingly important. But how does a determined leader do so with efficiency, sensitivity, and above all, legal compliance?

We have surveyed thousands of CEOs and key executives over the past few years. When we ask, "How many of you have at least one person on your team who is not living up to your expectations of success?" almost everyone raises a hand. The follow-up question reveals the real pain: "How long have you known this?"

What we hear shocks us as much today as it did five or six years ago, when we began asking these two questions in our workshops. We've had CEOs and key executives sheepishly hang their heads and respond, "Two years." "Six years." "Nine years."

Just last year, a CEO actually admitted his under-performer had been a conscious thorn in the company's side for *nineteen* years; even worse, it wasn't a family member.

Obviously, new managers who are struggling to adapt to their new position should not be hung out to dry, stranded without transition support, or mercilessly drummed out without discussion. But there is a huge difference between passively waiting for things to change and making a proactive effort to clarify expectations.

How To Clarify Expectations—The Right Way

At the end of the Introduction to this book, we introduced our Eight-Step Success Factor Methodology. The very first step of that process involves a unique tool that dramatically impacts and drives the entire hiring process.

That tool is the Success Factor Snapshot™.

In Chapter Six, you will learn a step-by-step process to build a detailed Success Factor Snapshot (SFS) for each position in your company. But we don't want to get ahead of ourselves. For now, all you need to know is that the SFS can also help you to deal with individuals in your organization who are faltering.

The SFS helps to reset and clarify expectations for currently under-performing employees, as well as identify issues that need to be addressed with existing executives.

Before you bring down the hatchet on a faltering employee, be sure they have all the information they need to succeed. Compare the "Description" below—a typical, nebulous mishmash of vague terms and fuzzy verbiage—with the Success Factor Snapshot that follows. Is it possible that an under-performer simply needs to understand expectations and objectives in a more concrete way?

Job Description

VP of Sales and Marketing

Position Summary

Reports to President and manages internal and external sales teams to increase company's sales growth in all major markets.

- Develop and implement strategic and tactical sales plans.
- Proactively develop new business opportunities that leverage company's technical capabilities.
- Coordinate internal resources to provide best-in-class pre- and post-sales service and support to our customers.

Responsibilities

- Responsible for overall performance of company's sales team and the continued expansion of sales of the company's product line of software/hardware development tools and boundary-scan test equipment.
- Development of new business and product opportunities for the company.
- Responsible for recruiting, managing, and coordinating efforts of independent rep firms and distributors in support of sales opportunities.
- Oversee marketing programs including management and implementation of demand creation programs, customer intelligence marketing, and customer communications programs.
- Conduct product presentations and demonstrations, online via the Web, at the customer's location and at industry meetings.
- Travel to customer sites for sales calls and technical presentations. Participate in industry trade shows and seminars as required.

Success Factor Snapshot

Vice President of Sales and Marketing

Success Factor 1: **Within twelve months, increase sales by 15% over the prior year.**

- Develop a tactical sales plan for the next fiscal year for existing markets and products within two months from which 50% of the increase in sales will be generated.
- Create within three months a plan of action to enter the telecommunications and medical device markets and achieve a goal of $6 million before the end of the next fiscal year, representing 25% of the sales objective.
- Effectively launch within four months a new product coming out of R&D now which represents a revolutionary advancement over competitor products. Effective launch will be defined as the product generating $6 million before the end of the next fiscal year.

Success Factor 2: **Implement a sales infrastructure to effectively manage the sales activities and process within twelve months.**

- Within one month, create a sales pipeline forecasting tool that is within 10% accuracy on a monthly basis.
- Within three months, develop a structured process for sales call tracking, reporting, weekly updates, and one-to-one meetings with each subordinate.
- Within six months, implement group and individual sales training. Develop a scorecard to measure each Regional Sales Manager in his or her sales ability and product knowledge.

Success Factor 3: **Develop a Strategic three-year plan ensuring 15% growth year-over-year beginning in next Fiscal Year.**

- Conduct a comprehensive product optimization review within three months. Identify products to be discontinued, new products to be added, and additional products requiring substantial engineering resources to upgrade/improve.
- Identify within six months at least one new market to enter in each fiscal year that will generate annualized revenues of at least $15 million at 15% EBIT.
- Conduct an acquisition study within twelve months to target potential acquisitions that will fill the gap between the 15% targeted growth rate and organic growth.

The Value of Clarity And The Necessity Of Strength

One of our clients was the CEO of a $60 million distribution business. Over lunch one day, he was lamenting the fact that his Chief Financial Officer's deficiencies were having detrimental effects on the company and the rest of the staff. When we asked how long this had been going on, the client replied, "A couple of years now." *Years?*

The problem was, our friend the CEO was a Really Nice Guy.

He had built his company from the ground up. The CFO had been with him from the start. How could he let go of someone, he asked, who had been there by his side from Day One, back when all they had was a big dream and an "operations center" that doubled as a two-car garage? But it was even worse, he said. Not only was the CFO a close confidante who had been through it all with him—she was also a single mother with a disabled child.

He acknowledged that her abilities and results were not as strong as they could be. In fact, she had made some costly mistakes. Still, he could not bear to think about firing her. It seemed downright wrong. Unethical, even.

We tried to help Really Nice Guy to understand that keeping her on, in a position that was obviously beyond her capabilities, was actually more "wrong." If the CFO's under-performance led to business failure, it would not only affect her livelihood and child, but also the livelihoods (and children) of many other people who were also employed by the company.

In the long run, he wasn't doing her—or the company—any favors. Allowing her to remain in a stressful position that created daily performance struggles created a threat to her own health and well being. Wouldn't it be better for her to find a position that allowed her to excel, take pride in her work, and provide for her child in the long run?

To help Really Nice Guy work up the clarity and strength to do what he needed to do, we led him through the process of developing a Success Factor Snapshot for the position. We asked him to list all the measurable results that he should reasonably expect from a CFO in a $60 million business.

By the time lunch was over, Really Nice Guy could finally see, in black and white, that keeping the CFO around was doing measurable harm to himself, his company, and other employees—even the CFO herself. But until he actually sat down, worked through the Success Factor Snapshot, and codified his expectations, he had no way of understanding the magnitude of the mismatch.

If you are reading this chapter and do not recognize any similarities to your own company, congratulations. You're a step ahead, and you can skip straight to the next section.

But if you are feeling a bit uncomfortable—if perhaps you are beginning to wonder about an employee or two (more?) who are currently under-performing—you are not alone.

If there are glaring examples of under-performance in your company right now, we urge you to lay out concrete, realistic expectations for the position. Creating a Success Factor Snapshot will help you to do just that. (Skip ahead to Chapter 6 to get right down to it.) This exercise should bring into sharp focus just how well your current employee is stacking up against a reasonable ideal.

As with our friend, Mr. Really Nice Guy CEO, laying things out in black and white can help to make the right decision crystal clear. But do you have the emotional resolve to follow through on what you know is right for your company?

Emotional Strength is One Hidden Key To Successful Management

Whether you are a Really Nice Guy or a Tough-As-Nails executive with a reputation for iron-fisted competence, you probably hate firing people. Outside of theft, embezzlement, or selling trade secrets to competitors, you would really rather "give them another chance." That is only human.

For most CEOs and key executives, having to fire someone is the most unpleasant thing they are faced with in a business setting. It's gut wrenching and causes sleepless nights.

An executive who wants to give an under-performer "a little more time" usually rationalizes inaction in one of the following ways:

- **"I Am SuperCoach!"** *Maybe you can coach an under-performing manager to achieve the results you expect. If you just spend more time with him…mentor her a bit more…send him to motivational seminars…invest a bit more in training… .* Perhaps, in a rare case, coaching would help. But more often than not, executives who have walked down this well-worn path can tell you that at the end of it, you will find the very same dead end. And you will have wasted precious time and money along the way.

- **"She's got it all—we can't lose!"** Your new VP of Marketing has it all. An MBA from Harvard Business School. Fifteen years of experience at your closest competitor during their rapid expansion. A long list of impressive credentials. You have it in your head that she is so talented, she cannot possibly fail. So, when results are not materializing—when the new product launch fails and your oldest product line is losing market share, too—you find it nearly impossible to believe. It can't be the superstar. It must be something else.

- **"He's my man!"** *You two go way back. You played ball together in college. He stood up for you at your wedding. Your kids wrestled together in the back yard during countless barbecues. You have been working together to build this company since he quit his day job to come work for you fifteen years ago.* Still. Blind loyalty and friendship should never cloud your judgment on performance. Even if you love to golf with the guy, his lack of performance is hurting your whole company.

- **"I don't want them to know I screwed up!"** *Could it be that the Board of Directors will decide you are the one who is not leading effectively if you don't cover for the non-performers? Isn't it safer to proceed as if nothing is wrong? What they don't know can be fixed with just a little more time. Right? Not to mention, you probably hired this person to start with.* Admitting that a hire was a mistake is tough. Almost as tough as watching the entire organization begin a slow-motion death spiral because you do not want to acknowledge and correct the problem...

- **"I can't have an empty desk."** *Well, OK, so the new hire is not getting much done, but some work is surely better than no work. Right? You do not want to be burdened with extra work while you spend more time and resources looking for yet another new hire.* Never mind that the cleanup operation will take even more time and money later...

Procrastination is the bad habit of putting off until the day after tomorrow what should have been done the day before yesterday.

Napoleon Hill

You Can't Afford To Wait If A Hire Is Not Working Out

If you are still inclined to offer an under-performer that third, fourth, or seventh chance, then it is time to revisit costs.

In Chapter 1, you filled out the "Cost of One Bad Hire" worksheet. If you are finding the prospect of firing College Friend Stan or Sally daunting, you might find it helpful to re-examine that worksheet, running the numbers specifically for your current ineffective executive. After you have identified reasonable expectations for the position, it will be easy to see what they are not living up to and what that costs your organization.

Chapter Summary

❖ **You must identify problem executives right away.** Whether it is a new hire or a promotion gone wrong, giving people "a little more time" may be more harmful than helpful.

❖ **Clearly define the expectations for the position.** Developing a Success Factor Snapshot (Chapter 6) for the problematic position will give you a means to measure and manage your executive's performance. Our advice is to do this up front to ensure success from the beginning, rather than trying to catch up later.

❖ **Examine the cost of giving the bad hire chance after chance.** Once you have clearly documented the direct costs and lost opportunity costs of your mediocre employee, take immediate action to identify and hire a Top 5% individual for that role. We guarantee you'll feel like a weight has been lifted from your shoulders.

SECTION 2: FORGET EVERYTHING YOU KNOW

Chapter 4: Hiring The Right Person ALWAYS Takes Too Long

> If you spend a lot of time figuring out who you're going to hire, you'll have to spend far less time figuring out who to fire.
>
> *Michael J. Lotito*

Doing It Fast vs. Getting It Right

Probably the most common complaint we hear is, "Hiring takes too long." We hear it from candidates and clients alike.

In books, articles, and placement offices around the country, impatient job seekers are frankly cautioned up front that the process is going to take longer than they would like it to. Usually a LOT longer.

Few people are quite so candid with hiring executives.

The CEO or President with a vacant desk in the corner office has his own set of pressures, demands, costs, and stresses. It is no wonder that leaders are in a hurry to fill vacancies. They would not be human otherwise.

So, we feel our clients' pain when we hear, "I need this job filled *fast.*" But we wouldn't be living up to our own code of business ethics if we used that as an excuse to treat a critical search in a superficial way.

The process of finding and hiring Top 5% Talent takes hard work, and that, in turn, takes time. It's best if everybody recognizes this fact at the outset.

The Hidden Lair Of Top 5% Talent: The Candidate Pyramid

When you are hiring and you want to find Top 5% Talent, you have a serious challenge on your hands. It's going to take time, and it's going to take patience. Top 5% Talent is not surfing the online job boards or looking through Help Wanted ads in trade publications. They are busy doing their job—and doing it well. Add to that the fact their current employer is usually doing everything to ensure they are happy and not considering greener pastures.

There are four basic pools of candidates that make up the complete spectrum of talent in every search.

- One pool—*Non-Candidates*—contains people who are never, ever going to join your firm (or anybody else's, either). They are staying where they are until the bitter end. Still, Non-Candidates can provide valuable leads from time to time, so they may be worth one phone call. This pool is made up of a variety of people: those who may be reaching retirement, those who just started work, those with an equity position or a family member employed at their current company, and so on.

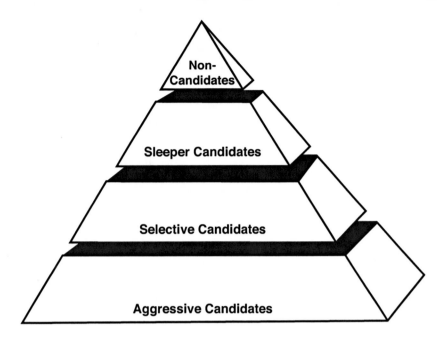

Non-Candidates
Not Open To Any Opportunity
Very settled in current position. A "lifer" or near-future retiree who is actively resistant to the possibility of change.

Sleeper Candidates
Unconsciously Open To a Better Opportunity
Successful and happy in current position. Not looking, no current resume, but open-minded. May initially be resistant. Can be brought around for a compelling opportunity and motivational factors. Requires professional sourcing and recruiting.

Selective Candidates
Consciously Open To a Better Opportunity
Employed and satisfied. May have a current resume. Checks job boards occasionally for compelling positions, but not actively pursuing a job change. Requires savvy recruiting. Critical source of Top 5% Talent.

Aggressive Candidates
Actively Seeking a New Position
May be unemployed or unhappy in current position. Actively seeking employment; applying for numerous positions, actively interviewing, eager to find a new job and may not be selective about the job or company. Responds to numerous ads hoping for a call. 80% of applicants; marginal source of Top 5% Talent.

- The next two groups—*Selective* and *Sleeper Candidates*—are usually the most difficult and costly to source. They are also the candidates who are *most worth finding*—the group that is most likely to contain Top 5% Talent. Other experts blend these two pools together, calling the whole crowd "passive candidates," but we know from experience these are two distinct groups. Each requires a different approach to find, recruit, persuade, and close. The critical difference is their level of *immediate openness* to the possibility of a new position.

  o A *Sleeper Candidate* may not even know she is open to a new opportunity until the third or fourth recruiting call. Sleeper Candidates are so good at what they do, so well rewarded, and so satisfied with their current position, they are busy creating a better opportunity right where they are. These candidates cannot simply be invited to apply for your position; they must be actively courted and wooed. There is a high probability that they have not updated their resume in years, because they have had no need to do so. When a Sleeper changes positions, it's usually because they were referred in. Their reputation precedes them. Sleepers, like high-strung racehorses, need careful, patient handling. Sometimes it takes four or five carefully constructed phone calls full of "What Ifs…" and "Suppose we coulds…" before they will consider putting together their resume. It might take an additional week or two for them to get the resume finished and round up references.

  o A *Selective Candidate* is immediately and consciously open to another position, but only if it is a *compelling* opportunity. This candidate occasionally wonders what else is out there for a person with his abilities, but only rarely acts on this. He may scan industry-specific ads once or twice a year; he keeps up with his network; he may even send off a resume now and again. But for the most part, he is not actively engaged with a job search. Companies can generally find these candidates through employee referral programs, and by networking with organizations, vendors, customers, and other groups that can get the word out about their opportunity. These methods, of course, are a very slow process. Word-of-mouth networking and referrals take time to find their way to that top candidate.

- The final type of candidate—the *Aggressive Candidate*—is the kind that the HR department hears from every day. These people are actively, enthusiastically on the market *right now*. They are entering or re-entering the job market. If currently employed, they have decided to leave their current company, or they know lay-offs are just around the corner. This group includes some Top 5% Talent; still, such people are snapped up in the blink of an eye and represent a small overall percentage of the pool. Aggressive Candidates are the most likely to try to be chameleons in the hiring process, to say whatever it is they think the hiring team wants to hear. They are the most likely candidates to turn into somebody else when they begin the job, leaving the employer to lament, "You're not the person I hired!" By far, the bulk of readily available applicants for every open position are Aggressive Candidates. They are applying to anything that remotely suits them—after all, they need a job.

If your desire is to attract and hire Top 5% Talent, we can provide a framework to build a hiring system that methodically identifies, contacts, and invites the top sources of hidden talent—Selective and Sleeper Candidates. They are harder to find and harder to hire, but they are worth every dollar spent and every bit of effort required.

Do Not Believe Empty Promises

Unlike the typical job seeker, who usually has plenty of people around him willing to tell him the Truth That Hurts, corporate leaders are often cursed with flattery, smooth talkers, and just plain bad counsel.

There is never a shortage of yes-men who are willing to come into the boardroom and promise things that simply are not possible. "Sure, Sir, we can fill that vacant COO position in six weeks. Trust us."

Well, maybe they *can* fill a COO position in six weeks. But whom are they going to fill it with? The chances are high that any hire based on speed and expediency is going to prove to be a long-term disaster.

A fast search is by necessity a *superficial search*. It will begin and end, of necessity, with the majority coming from the Aggressive Candidate pool.

The chances of finding the *right* Top 5% candidate from that pool is about the same as your chance of stumbling into Caesar's Palace, sinking your last dollar into the great big slot machine near the front door, and winning the biggest jackpot in Vegas history. Sure, it could happen. But it's not likely.

A fast search is not going to tap into the full spectrum of candidates. It simply cannot.

But What About All Those Guys Out There Who Say They Can Get Really Fast Results?

Let's separate myth from reality.

The Myth. There is an Executive Search Wizard who has great powers—powers beyond those of mere mortals.

If you hire The Executive Search Wizard to do your next executive search, he will reach into his Magic Hat (read: "Big fat database"), pull out five perfectly qualified candidates within a week or two, and present them to you. Fairy dust will rain down from the heavens. You will select your favorite interviewee in Week Three. You will make an offer on Monday of Week Four. On Monday of Week Six, without even a day off between jobs, your new Perfect Employee will be seated in his corner office at your workplace, ready to move mountains, triple profits, and bring homemade cookies to the entire staff. The Wizard's job is done, and he collects his well-earned check.

The Reality. Rome was not built in a day. You cannot fabricate a Lamborghini in twenty minutes. Bordeaux takes years to mature. And a short *successful* search is rare.

We try to avoid blanket statements, but we will make an exception here. *If a recruiter tells you they can complete a systematic, detail-oriented, well-sourced, thoroughly successful executive or managerial search in six to eight weeks, every hair on the back of your neck should stand up and you should get that guarantee in writing.* We feel strongly about this point, because over the course of twenty years, we have heard too many tales of seductive sales pitches that promised speed above all else—and ultimately led to nightmare hires. Too often, we have had to do "cleanup duty" after a disastrous hire because the hiring executive was seduced by a false promise and prioritized speed above all else.

No matter how much our potential clients might want to hear "We can do that search in six weeks," the reality is a systematic, well-sourced search takes time.

An Inescapable Fact. A highly effective, successful search is going to take *on average* fourteen weeks, depending on a wide variety of factors.

- Does the company have an adequate position description based on success factors (or whether one needs to be built from scratch)?

- How specialized are the requirements? Could a lot of people fill the job, or just a handful nationwide? Worldwide?

- How accessible are potential candidates to find? Do they spend their days behind security fences, sitting in bomb-proof bunkers a half-mile below the desert, designing weapons systems? Or are they out slapping backs and shaking hands at networking events?

- How flexible are the company and the candidates (geography, relocation, compensation, benefits, etc.)?

- Will candidates be traveling to interviews?

- How many company executives will interview each candidate? Will there be panel interviews? How many rounds of interviews will there be?

- What interim details need to be defined? Will the candidate be expected to do a presentation? And if so, to whom?

- Will complex legal paperwork be involved in finalizing the hire?

- Does the candidate have an existing contract? And are you willing to deal with this type of issue to hire the best?

- How deep does the background check need to be?

For a shorter search, something's got to give. It's up to the hiring executive to decide what he or she is willing to forfeit.

There is always a tradeoff between getting a search done quickly and fishing in deep waters. One of the ten top hiring mistakes in our study (see Appendix 2) is that companies do not invest enough time to source "selective" and "sleeper" candidates. In a quick search, Aggressive candidates make up a vast majority of the pool, entirely missing the most likely source of Top 5% Talent.

"But I Need This Position Filled Faster Than That!"

When we tell people the hard truth about how long a successful hire takes, the first thing we can count on hearing is, "I don't have time for that" or, "We can't wait that long to get someone in here."

Ideally, no hiring executive would wait until an actual vacancy occurs to begin a new search. In a perfect world, everybody would plan far ahead. Searches for a December vacancy would begin in April.

But if a vacancy already exists, and speed really *is*, for whatever reason, the number one criterion for filling a job, we tell prospective clients they have three choices.

1. Conduct a lightning-fast but cursory search of Aggressive Candidates whose resumes are immediately available on a variety of Internet sites. Invite the top few who emerge from this pack in for an interview. Hire the best of the bunch. Cross your fingers and hope that things work out.

This kind of search can be finished in a month.

If things go well, great. You lucked out. If not, the cleanup after this kind of hire can take a year or more.

Just like winning the lottery, it is *possible* to hire Top 5% Talent this way. It just isn't probable.

2. Do a limited search through multiple search firms, all of which forward a slew of resumes, which in turn are box-checked against a standard job description. Each firm hopes that of the twelve resumes they sent, perhaps you will fall in love with one. Spend a great deal of internal time reviewing resumes and interviewing people who turn out to be unqualified. *This kind of search can be wrapped up in eight to ten weeks.* The results are generally not much

49

better than the results of a scattershot Aggressive Candidate search under option one, but at least you have a chance of seeing some selective candidates. (Many of our clients have been frustrated in the past by traditional search firms who place the same advertising the client company could have, but still expect a large fee.)

3. Take a deep breath, swallow your objections, hold your horses, and commit to fixing your hiring process now, once and for all. Invest the time it takes to base your next hire on the kind of performance you expect. Invest several weeks in the Success Factor Methodology. It will guide not only the new hire, but also the entire company in years to come.

In other words, if you are committed to hiring Top 5% Talent, there is no shortcut. Companies that thrive end up figuring this out, one way or another. Organizations that take the "quick and dirty" way out inevitably do the same searches over and over again.

We truly wish we had a wizard's hat and a magical database. But the truth is that nobody—*nobody*—does.

The following graphic can help you to understand the scope of a truly comprehensive search. Depending on the level of the position and the complexities of expected performance, it may take screening *300 or more Aggressive, Selective and Sleeper candidates* to come up with the Top 5% of Talent to interview.

The Success Factor Methodology Hiring Funnel

All Candidates (300-500)
· Screen all resumes from Aggressive Candidates
· Identify and recruit Selective & Sleeper Candidates
· Eliminate 95%+ for obvious mismatches

Preliminary Candidates (25-100)
· Phone screen and interviews
· Disqualify bottom 95%

Finalist Candidates (2-3)
· Interview top 5% in depth
· Check references
· Assessments & homework

HIRE

Desperation Hiring: A Recipe For Failure

Several years back, we ran across a CEO with a bad case of impatience. The company, a small textile firm with revenues in the $25 million neighborhood, needed a Chief Information Officer to move the organization through rapid changes in the technology end of the business. There was no HR department. The CEO himself had been directly hiring and firing for years.

He had found the previous CIO through a shallow search—an ad in the local paper, a pool of Aggressive Candidates, a quick offer to the one who appeared most qualified.

When we met with the CEO, things were (predictably) not working out. He had let the CIO go and was reopening the search.

But he had learned *nothing* from his previous rush to hire. Once again, he wanted somebody in that chair RIGHT NOW.

We leveled with the CEO about how long it would take to find not just any candidate, but the *right* candidate who could deliver the success he needed. We told him, realistically, taking into account the challenges the new CIO would face, he should expect the hiring process to take three to four months.

His response was, "I do not have three months."

He hired a contingency recruiting firm who told him what he wanted to hear—they promised to fill the job within two months. And so they did.

Six months later, we were called back in. The quick hire hadn't worked out. We didn't say, "I told you so."

We started all over, from scratch, and we completed a deep search, the *right way,* using the Success Factor Methodology. By the time we placed a strong candidate, it was *nine months down the road* from that first poor hire.

So, the CEO who thought he "did not have three months" to fill a critical leadership position ended up wasting a total of nine months, steep search fees, and a lot of productivity. All because he was unwilling to face the hard truth up front—a great hire takes time.

The good news is, the CIO we placed with that client has been with the company ever since. For nearly a decade, he has shepherded the company's information systems through streamlining, platform changes, three company moves, rapid expansion, addition of product lines, and the launch of new systems that improved the bottom line.

Investing "extra" time up front to make sure you find the right candidate pays off in multiples down the road.

When you are tempted to rush a hire, think in terms of Return on Investment over the course of years, not months. Everyone is looking for a magic bullet that will make hiring quick and painless. In our experience, there is no magic bullet when you are conducting a search for a critical role. It takes hard work and can amount to 150-300 hours of networking, sourcing, discussions, negotiations, and so on to find the Top 5% Talent who can succeed.

Chapter Summary

❖ **Just like job hunters,** hiring executives need to budget realistic amounts of time—and effort—for results-oriented searches

❖ **Four types of workers** comprise the total talent pool for every position:
  ➤ Non-candidates
  ➤ Sleeper Candidates
  ➤ Selective Candidates
  ➤ Aggressive Candidates

❖ **Thorough searches must reach Selective and Sleeper Candidates** as well as Aggressive ones

❖ **Finding the Top 5% may require screening 300+** people for an open position

❖ **Desperation Hiring doesn't work.** Investing in a proven system to find the right person will actually save time, money and deliver desired results in years ahead.

Chapter 5: Traditional Job Descriptions Are Worthless

> Too often, hiring is a process frequently conducted by people with only a tenuous grasp of the work the candidate is being considered for.
>
> *Tom Peters*

What Should Go Into The Job Description? That's The Last Of Your Worries

The frustrations that plague most business leaders are surprisingly similar, no matter what the industry, product, service, price point, or annual revenues. These frustrations are common, but CEOs who take the time to determine clear organizational objectives and tie them to each executive's performance expectations ensure flawless execution as they pursue their vision and strategy.

In order to hire effectively, CEOs must first step back and get a full view of the "big picture."

In most job searches, the first flurry of activity is to develop a job description. But that should be the last of a hiring team's worries. Overall business strategy, vision, the annual operating plan, and interdependencies among these lead directly to the construction of a useful job description—not the other way around.

A Case In Point

We recently sat down with a client who wanted to find a new Director of Human Resources for a $40 million manufacturing business. The hiring team came into the room with the notion that the meeting's purpose was to "write up the job description." We knew there would be a lot more work to do than that.

Through the course of the meeting, we discovered (as we often do) that the team had serious issues to address before they could even *begin* to think about a job specification.

They needed to step back—way back—and begin with a top-level view of the organization's goals.

- We asked what the short- and long-term plan was for the business.

- We asked how the new executive's accomplishments would support and affect the overall goals of the company.

- We asked how the new director's objectives aligned with the other departmental objectives.

- We probed to find out what specific initiatives the new hire would be expected to execute.

- We pressed to discover what resources and obstacles would shape the new hire's performance in the first year.

We weren't surprised to hear that the hiring team hadn't thought about how the objectives linked with this position. Almost none of our clients over the past twenty years have.

And yet, for a search to be successful, that level of strategic thinking and groundwork is absolutely critical.

When we asked the CEO of this organization how he intended to set goals for the new Director of Human Resources, he was vague: "We expect to see a significant increase in employee development, and we will sit down with the new person once they come on board and go over some targets."

A primary key to success in hiring is a strong linkage between organizational goals and individual goals.

The Success Factor Methodology ensures that clients clearly define expectations for their new executive hire and that those expectations are tied directly into the organizational goals. Our experience in more than a thousand executive searches over the last twenty years is when our clients use this systematic process, they significantly increase accuracy in hiring executives who deliver upon their expectations. Without considering these issues, there is a high probability that the company will fall prey to the 56% failure rate discussed in Chapter One.

The Domino Effect

The Success Factor Methodology is, at its core, a structured set of tools to help business leaders envision and define success at all levels of the company in concrete, measurable terms. It is an approach that translates vision into action in a chain reaction, just like tumbling dominos.

One large "domino"—corporate goals—sets up and drives every action down the chain, across the entire company. If the first domino is not appropriately set, the chain reaction cannot begin. If subsequent dominos are misaligned, the chain reaction stops. Only complete alignment leads to success.

Once our clients envision hiring success as a manifestation of the Domino Effect, it becomes apparent that hiring is not simply a matter of replacing an outgoing Controller, Marketing Director, or VP of Operations. Each position *does* have individual goals, but they are driven by larger departmental goals and ultimately by the company goals.

Consider that a "problem in sales" may not *actually* be a problem in sales at its root. It could be that a sales slump is actually the result of lagging product development. Perhaps there has been no new product introduction lately. If that is the case, then replacing the Director of Sales will not necessarily solve the "sales" problem. You'll have to look elsewhere to fix the leak.

Probing deeper may even reveal higher-level problems. Product Development may also not hold the key to solving the problem. Perhaps their prototypes are languishing, awaiting "go-ahead" in dark rooms strung with red tape. The real root of the problem may be Legal. Or Manufacturing. Or late deliveries by key vendors. Or possibly a materials shortage due to financing problems.

A business, like an engine, is an enormous system made up of a great number of interdependent parts. Each part affects the working of the entire engine. If just *one* piston or crankshaft or combustion reaction is out of sync with the rest, performance suffers.

Before a business leader can build a powerful, efficient engine, he or she must be able to step back and envision which parts are needed, how they fit together, and what they should ultimately produce.

Trickle-Down Goals: Individual Positions Come Last

Not linking organizational goals with position goals is a recipe for failure.

Most often, when we begin engagements, our clients want to skip right over high-level goals. "We have a strategic plan," they'll say, and point to the highest shelf in the room at a document that's been created with the best of intentions. But plan implementation has been left to subordinates. Senior management and department heads do not act to execute the plan; they become mere cheerleaders who exhort their employees to somehow make it happen.

And then they wonder what went wrong as a VP is asked to leave because his department's goals were not accomplished in the allotted time period.

The truth is, most companies cause their own pain in the hiring process. Two typical scenarios: a functional executive is on the way out, or a position has been open too long. Work is piling up, customers are screaming, and critical projects are falling through the cracks. Frustration and desperation causes the hiring team to attempt to shorten the hiring process.

Without a firm grasp on overall organizational goals, results from a new hire are likely to be random—even counterproductive. How can you expect a new hire to deliver goals that are not defined prior to hiring the candidate?

In our workshops and for every search, we teach our clients to begin the hiring process by specifically stating overall company goals for the next twelve to eighteen months.

Sometimes those goals are monetary; sometimes they involve launching and completing a critical project; sometimes they involve increasing market share, opening a new branch of business, spinning off divisions, or acquiring other companies.

Knowing what you want to accomplish is the only way to designate meaningful, measurable sub-goals for employees.

Managing goals throughout the organization is a cascading operation that moves objectives downward through the organization. Individual position goals are the last to be specified, based on input from higher-level goals. The Success Factor Methodology ensures that this happens in the right order.

Success Factor Linkage™ (SFL)

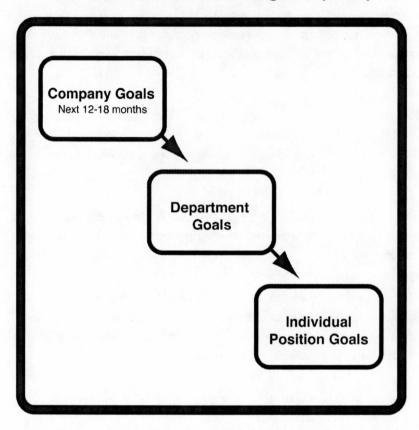

Once organizational goals are established through some form of strategic or business planning, the next step is to link them to functional area goals in order to create position goals.

We call this alignment of cascading goals the Success Factor Linkage™ (SFL).

In The Same Boat, Rowing In Different Directions

Many of our clients, past and present, have told us they are frustrated by "silo mentality" in their organizations. Turf wars and political intrigue are so common that many people think of them as "normal."

The first thing we try to impress upon our clients is that these are *not* normal. Interdepartmental squabbling and infighting are signs of a team that doesn't see the whole vision. The company's goals are not yet crystal clear.

Functional department heads must understand that they, like rowers, are all in the same boat, and if they want to move out of the center of the lake, they're going to have to row together. Otherwise, they can't help but row in circles.

Recently, we placed a new Vice President of Sales in an organization that had refused to initially invest the time and energy to develop Success Factor Linkage. The results were nearly disastrous.

Within three months, the newly placed candidate was calling us, saying, "I made a mistake. I have to get out of here." To make a long story short, he had become a pawn in a vicious power struggle between the Vice President of Operations and the President of the company. While the President's directives and mandate for the new Sales VP were clear, the VP of Operations was threatened by the new employee's initiatives; the "old guard" launched a pitched battle to protect his turf.

Without a clear view of shared overall goals, the VP of Operations had forgotten that they were all in the same boat.

As a result, he refused to acknowledge that "his turf" was only a small piece of the larger organizational puzzle, and that every company executive had the right and the responsibility to suggest adjustments and improvements that would boost the overall bottom line.

Ultimately, after six months of the power struggle, the President relieved the obstructionist VP of Operations. The CEO contacted us to replace the outgoing VP of Operations. This time, we insisted on developing SFL before we began an active search.

We conducted an in-house training program for the management team to ensure everyone was at same starting point and to build consensus about the need for SFL.

Only then was the new Sales VP finally free to implement the plans and strategies he had generated to meet his functional departmental goals—and by extension, organizational goals. He flourished, and in turn, so did the organization, which was finally aligned from the top down.

Traditional "Job Descriptions" Are Worthless

In trainings, speeches, and engagements with clients, we start by shattering common assumptions about hiring. One of those assumptions is that job descriptions are useful documents in the hiring process. We contend that job descriptions are completely worthless.

"What do you mean, worthless? How can anybody hire with no job description? You're crazy."

Allow us to clarify.

We don't mean that job descriptions have no value as legal or archival documents. They are worthless *for hiring Top Talent.*

Traditional job descriptions *do not* help you:

- align organizational goals with departmental goals or individual position goals
- create a roadmap for the hiring process
- clarify expectations
- generate a compelling marketing statement that will attract Top 5% Talent
- determine the best Sourcing Strategy to find and attract Top Talent
- assess and verify the quality and depth of a candidate's track record
- manage ongoing performance of a new hire

Traditional job descriptions simply lump together an amalgam of skills, knowledge, abilities, attributes, responsibilities, years of experience, education, and behavioral adjectives—none of which are consistent predictors of on-the-job success.

In our survey, *The Top Ten Hiring Mistakes*, we discovered that the number one hiring mistake is using an inadequate job description to guide the hiring process.

We've developed a much better tool that outshines a traditional job description—the Success Factor Snapshot™.

What's Really Driving Your Hiring Processes?

The norm in most organizations is to specify, via a traditional job description, the *minimum* a candidate must have in order to apply for the job: Minimum education, minimum years in the industry, minimum experience, minimum skills, minimum knowledge. It is a description of a person, rather than a description of the position.

The end result is a piece of paper that makes Human Resources and Legal happy, but is not at all useful for hiring Top Talent who will help achieve the company's goals.

The harsh reality is, when you *define a job* in mediocre terms, you tend to *attract and interview* mediocre people.

It's a good thing professional sports teams don't build their rosters using traditional job descriptions. Shrewd coaches know it doesn't matter how much an athlete can bench press, what school he attended, how fast he can swing the bat, how far he can throw the ball, or how many years he has been in the league. These and other "qualifications" are static traits in isolation; they describe bits and pieces of the athlete, this is not to say they aren't important skills, but they do not predict whether he will be able to effectively *use* those traits in the game situation to put the pigskin between the uprights, the puck in the net, or a ball over the outfield wall.

What counts most, in both sports *and* business, is not what traits you bring to the game, but what you can *accomplish* by using those traits. The coach cares whether an athlete can deliver results and help the team to *win*.

That is why coaches rely on scouts. The scout observes the athlete in the game, focusing solely on his or her ability to perform on the job with the rest of the team.

The Success Factor Methodology takes a coach's perspective on hiring. It moves hiring out of the realm of static traits and into the realm of action and results.

Our research led to the development of the Success Factor Snapshot (SFS), which is the cornerstone of our methodology. This document, which replaces the traditional job description, is a tool that breaks down a position's requirements in terms of *specific, measurable deliverables, benchmarks, and timetables.*

The SFS is the glue that holds all the goals of an organization together. Ideally, organizations should ultimately create Success Factor Snapshots for *every* position in the organization, because each SFS ties individual performance into the organization's objectives.

If you take nothing else away from this book, take this: **The single most critical thing you can do to improve your hiring process is to use the SFS to align all your company's cascading goals.**

From Company Goals To A Success Factor Snapshot: An Overview

The next chapter outlines *how* to create a SFS, but first, we want you to understand *why* doing so is important.

The following diagram shows the central position of the SFS within the organization's management systems. The SFS is the "hub" around which everything else revolves.

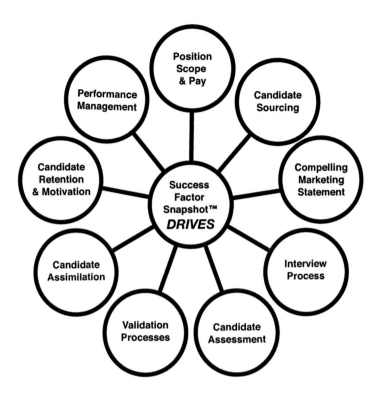

Position Scope And Pay. The SFS makes it much easier to define an open position in terms of the candidate you need, not the skills and experience he or she has assembled through the years. In a surprising number of cases, we've found that hiring executives are attempting to hire somebody whose expected scope of work and deliverables does not match the job level of the open position. Based on a more concrete understanding of expectations and results, the SFS drives what the level, compensation, and scope of the job should be—not the other way around.

Candidate Sourcing. The process of putting together a SFS can greatly help as you develop a sourcing strategy. It prompts you to think about where you should look to attract a larger pool of Top Talent.

Compelling Marketing Statement. This document goes far beyond just replacing the traditional tools used to advertise a position. The Compelling Marketing Statement uses the SFS as the core of portraying the job as a compelling opportunity. Top Talent will more readily raise their hand and come forward upon seeing the opportunity described in terms of the specific impact they will have on the organization vs. the traditional approach, which represents an arbitrary listing of skills, past experience, duties, and responsibilities. (See examples on our Web site, www.impacthiringsolutions.com.)

Interview Process. Putting together a SFS gives you a built-in structure for interviews, helping your hiring team focus 100% on what needs to be done. Success Factors also provide the substance for several core interview questions that ensure a high-quality, equitable interview process.

Candidate Assessment. We have created an Eight-Dimension Success Matrix that allows the interviewing team to compare each candidate. This tool focuses on a candidate's ability to deliver results comparable to those defined in the SFS. In addition, it helps the hiring team to conduct a fair and objective comparison. (You can download an electronic version of this form from our Web site.)

Validation Process. When reference callers and fact-checkers are wrapping up the last details prior to the offer, the SFS leads to a final, specific set of verification questions. These ensure that the candidate being offered the position can actually accomplish the specified goals.

Candidate Assimilation. Because expectations are absolutely clear before the candidate begins work, the SFS allows a new hire to hit the ground running, even with very little direction, confident that he or she knows exactly what needs to be done. Adaptability is one of the five key issues to ensuring you've hired the right person. Clarifying and interviewing for defined expectations will provide a smoother transition and candidate assimilation.

Candidate Retention and Motivation. When high-caliber employees understand what is expected of them and see how their measurable accomplishments impact the overall organization, they are intrinsically motivated to continue on a path that offers them challenge and professional fulfillment. No more is the Director of Sales "Responsible for all sales activities in the Western Region": she is "Growing revenues by 23% in the next two years by developing 30 new channels and expanding retail locations by 150 in Washington, Oregon, California, and Nevada."

Performance Management. The SFS is the driving force for managing the performance of an individual employee. It provides the vehicle for coaching and objective discussions around performance, both on a monthly basis and in annual performance reviews.

A solid SFS is the beginning of a whole new way of looking at the organization. Creating the SFS requires a firm grasp of the overall company vision for the months and years ahead.

56% Failure Rate Cure

To review Chapter 1, four primary reasons for the 56% failure rate of new executives are:

- Focusing on irrelevant experience and skills
- Nebulous expectations
- Failure to clearly communicate expectations up front
- Flawed hiring processes

The SFS addresses these issues head-on. It eliminates irrelevant experiences and skills from the equation; it clarifies expectations; the new hire knows what is expected prior to coming on board; and, it starts the hiring process down the right path. We guide our clients to embrace the SFS as the starting point in their hiring process. Once the SFS methodology is embedded in their hiring process, not only will the company's hiring success rate increase significantly, but also the ability to achieve organizational objectives will substantially improve.

Chapter Summary

❖ **The Job Description is the last thing a hiring executive should think about—not the first.** Before individual goals can be spelled out, the company's goals must be crystal clear.

❖ **Individual position goals are the result of Success Factor Linkage**—a trickle-down motion that begins at the top of the organization, extends to departmental goals, and finally ends with specific position goals.

❖ **You get what you define.** If job descriptions focus on minimums, you will in all likelihood attract people who can achieve only the minimum.

❖ **The Success Factor Methodology and Success Factor Snapshot** (SFS) are tools that require up-front thinking about overall company goals. While such analysis may seem peripheral to filling an empty post, in point of fact it is absolutely critical.

❖ **The SFS drives a company's management systems.** The SFS is the hub connecting the interdependencies within the organization.

Chapter 6: Building A Success Factor Snapshot

> The most effective people begin with the end in mind.
>
> *Steven Covey*

SOARing To Success: A Project Management Approach To Hiring Success

If ever you have undertaken a sizeable endeavor like painting your house, you have already used every skill you will ever need to revolutionize your hiring process.

When the goal is large, the obstacles are many, and the timing is critical, we tend instinctively to approach projects in a step-by-step, manageable sequence, breaking down the larger goal into smaller, "bite-sized" pieces.

A smart painter does not begin the day with a fresh bucket of paint and a brand new brush in her hand. First, she must do a good deal of preparation: scraping, patching, sanding, removing outlet covers and hardware, taping off of areas that should not be painted, and finally priming. Only *then* can the new color be applied.

While large tasks can be approached without advance preparation, the outcomes would be (obviously) inferior. So it is with hiring.

The Success Factor Methodology applies project management techniques to hiring by taking what most businesses already do as a "natural" part of business, then applying those same techniques (management by objectives, deadlines, forecasting, marketing, research, managing resources, etc.) to the overall goal.

What Are Success Factors?

The core of the Success Factor Methodology is the Success Factor Snapshot (SFS), which replaces the traditional job description and completely drives all of the hiring processes. This unique document ties an individual's success directly to the organization's operating plan.

The SFS pulls together concise statements of important interim accomplishments called "Success Factors" for which a position-holder will be held accountable at the end of a specific period—usually twelve to eighteen months. In most executive and managerial positions, six to eight Success Factors are critical to success within such a timeframe.

Building A Success Factor Snapshot

First, the entire hiring team needs to willfully set aside the generic, one-size-fits-all job description that lurks in the HR files.

There is a very good chance that the entire organization has changed since the first person put together the original job description. Besides, job descriptions are historical artifacts. They describe the past, not the future. And isn't that where you want to go?

The Success Factor Snapshot is created using a methodology we call "SOAR"—**S**ubstantial departmental goal, **O**bstacles, **A**ction, **R**esults.

How To SOAR

Even though executives are, almost without exception, skilled at strategizing and planning for large-scale initiatives within their organization, we have found that they sometimes struggle with defining work in a way that is concrete, measurable, and directly related to overall company objectives.

In our retained search, workshops, and consulting, we use the SOAR Methodology and a structured template (The Success Factor Worksheet™) to facilitate the process of creating Success Factors. This template is available for downloading on our Web site (www. impacthiringsolutions.com). Below is a more detailed description of the SOAR methodology with a few examples for each element of the acronym:

Substantial Departmental Goal	Objectives that each department must achieve in order for the company's annual operating plan to be realized. *Examples:* • Improve On-Time Deliveries from 83% to 95% • Obtain a 15% cost reduction • Increase revenue in the Southwest Region from $11 million to $14 million
Obstacles	Barriers that the Departmental Executive or Manager must overcome to achieve the Substantial Departmental Goals. Issues, conditions, relationships, phenomena, problems, etc. that stand in the way • *Examples:* Low machine utilization • No mid-year budget revision for cost targets • Lack of new markets for existing products in the Southwest Territory
Action	Steps or activities required to overcome the obstacles *Examples:* • Improve machine utilization • Create a mid-year revised budget • Identify new markets for existing products in the Southwest Territory

Results	Quantifiable and time-based outcomes that will clearly indicate whether a person has succeeded or failed to meet the specific position goals. *Examples:* <ul><li>Improve machine utilization from 45% to 75% within 9 months</li><li>Create a mid-year revised budget within 90 days representing a 15% across-the-board cost reduction</li><li>Identify 3 new markets for existing products in the Southwest Territory that will generate $3 million of additional revenue within 12 months</li></ul>

Below is the step-by-step process we use when creating a Success Factor Snapshot.

Step One (S)	Assemble the entire hiring team. Begin with the annual operating plan. Identify the three to four **S**ubstantial departmental goals that must be accomplished over the next 12 to 18 months in order for the department to achieve its portion of the operating plan.
Step Two (OAR)	For each **S**ubstantial departmental goal, define two or three short-term **O**bstacles that must be overcome by the executives or managers in the department to achieve the goals. Identify concrete **A**ctions that must be taken to resolve the obstacles. Define measurable, time-based **R**esults.
Step Three	The **OAR**s together represent the individual's Success Factors that when achieved, ensure the department meets its goals. Consolidate the **O**bstacles, **A**ctions, and **R**esults into one coherent statement: A *Success Factor.*
Step Four	Compile the Success Factors into a Success Factor Snapshot for the position.

SOAR In Action: A Real-Life Example

We were retained to conduct a search for a VP of Operations.

Step One

S—Substantial Departmental Goal: We started by sitting down with the CEO and the hiring team and asking, "Based on your annual operating plan for the upcoming year, what is the manufacturing department's most *substantial goal?*"

The CEO's first answer was, "We are losing customers because of poor manufacturing efficiencies."

Although the statement was true, what the CEO described was a symptom—not the core problem. We pressed on.

By asking a series of questions, we helped the CEO pinpoint the actual goal: "Manufacturing must increase on-time deliveries to 98% within one year." Compare this statement with the CEO's first response, which failed to define what needed to happen in order to stop losing customers and achieve the departmental goals.

Step Two

O—Obstacles: With the substantial departmental goal clearly defined, we next asked the CEO, "In order to achieve this, what are the *obstacles* that have to be overcome?"

The CEO mentioned several obstacles standing in the way of on-time delivery. One key issue was unresolved conflicts of interest between the Purchasing department (which was rewarded for driving down material costs) and the Manufacturing department (which was expected to provide high quality products and was unwilling to risk scrapping entire production runs due to defective materials).

On the worksheet, the **O** became *"Raw material Price/Quality tradeoffs are not being managed effectively."*

A—Action: Our next question was, "What *action* would remedy this situation?"

The CEO let out a big sigh and replied, "That's a no-brainer. We need to develop and implement a strong vendor qualification program. We've tried before, but nobody here has ever actually successfully completed one." Good—now we were getting somewhere. On the Success Factor Worksheet, the **A** became *"Design and implement a vendor qualification program."*

R—Results: Finally, we asked, "What are the *results* you expect in order to consider a vendor qualification program a success?"

This question required considerable discussion. We pressed the CEO to come up with very specific numbers, benchmarks, and timelines.

Fifteen minutes later, the CEO wrapped up his thinking: *"A successful vendor qualification program should be implemented within six months, with zero defects and a commitment to 100% on-time delivery by vendors."* This statement by the CEO became the **R** on the Success Factor Worksheet.

Step Three

With that final piece in place, the Success Factor was finished. It represented just *one* of the future VP of Operations' individual goals:

> *Develop and implement within six months a vendor qualification program that would ensure zero defects and 100% on-time deliveries of raw materials.*

Step Four

We repeated the process, working through the SOAR methodology until each Success Factor was completely defined. Then we compiled them all into a comprehensive Success Factor Snapshot, which appears at the end of this chapter.

The entire discussion took a couple of hours and some hard analysis by the CEO.

Now we were ready to begin the search for a new VP of Operations who could achieve the Success Factor Snapshot.

Note that it took almost a *full hour* for the CEO and the hiring team to hash out just the *first* Success Factor. You should expect to invest the same amount of time—even more if you do not have an experienced guide to walk you and your hiring team through SOAR.

Traditional Job Descriptions vs. SFS

To demonstrate the difference between traditional job descriptions (actually provided to us by clients) and Success Factor Snapshots, we've included two examples.

As you read and compare, pay particular attention to the specific details in the SFS vs. the traditional job descriptions' focus on responsibilities, skills, knowledge, abilities, and a laundry list of vague terms.

Traditional Job Description

Vice President of Operations

Growing manufacturing company is seeking an experienced Vice President of Operations. Reporting directly to the CEO, this position is responsible for the overall management of production, inventory, distribution/shipping, and warehousing. The role will include overseeing the total budget for manufacturing and operations, and supervision of all staff through six key reports. This individual will also be responsible for formulating and implementing all manufacturing and operational policies.

Duties and Responsibilities

- Coordinates activities of Production management personnel. Motivates, hires, trains, and provides leadership to insure subordinates are properly trained and employee relation activities are addressed in a timely manner.
- Assists and directly supervise sister companies Production, Scheduling Manager, and Distribution Manager.
- Ensures that this team assists and/or supervises Plant Managers in directing, planning, and controlling the activities in production and distribution to insure that only the highest quality products are produced, in the most cost-effective manner consistent with customer needs and budgeted goals.
- Works with management to insure that plant products are produced with consistency and comply with government regulations and safety requirements.
- Coordinates with CEO, VP Finance, VP Treasurer, VP Sales and Plant Management all capital, budgeting, and reporting needs for the production facilities.
- Works with other functional departments to develop programs/ procedures to consistently improve quality, safety, cost, and customer service.
- Participates as a key member of the Management Team in setting overall company direction and goals.
- Develops plans for the efficient use of materials, machines, and staff resource allocation.
- Reviews production costs and product quality, and modified production and inventory control programs to maintain and enhance the profitable operation of each plant.

- Works with Senior Management in coordinating production, distribution, and warehousing in accordance with principles, policies, and procedures established by the company and all regulatory agencies.
- Reviews and communicates budgeted numbers with plant management on an ongoing basis.

Education/Experience/Job Training

Position typically requires a BA/BS degree and 10+ years of direct senior management experience within a manufacturing environment. Minimum five years' knowledge in the industry required. Demonstrated ability to effectively manage and direct exempt/professional level personnel required. Excellent verbal and written communication skills required.

Success Factor Snapshot

Vice President of Operations

Success Factor 1: **Within 12 months, improve on-time deliveries from 90% to 98%.**

- Develop and implement, within six months, a vendor qualifications program that will achieve zero defects and 100% on-time deliveries.
- Within three months, improve machine utilization to 98%.
- Within three months, implement quality controls and procedures to ensure less than 2% defects.

Success Factor 2: **Consolidate plant operations within 18 months**

- Within three months, develop and present to CEO a plan to consolidate two plants with no down time.
- Within four months, complete the new plant layout which includes work cells for all manufacturing processes.
- Within nine months, have the first cells up and running and producing at levels prior to move.

Success Factor 3: **Reduce manufacturing costs by 10%**

- Conduct a SWOT analysis in first three months and present a plan of action to reduce costs 10% based on this analysis.
- Within six months, reduce machine setup time by 30%.
- Identify main drivers of overtime and within six months present a plan that will address these issues and a timeframe to eliminate them.

Traditional Job Description

Title: Chief Financial Officer

Reports to: President

Number of reports: Four direct exempt and 15 non-exempt

Position Summary: This position is responsible for all accounting, finance, treasury and IT functions within the company.

Responsibilities:

- Responsible for annual budget process
- Responsible for the oversight of the information systems department including ERP system, corporate networks, telecommunications and strategy
- Contribute to corporate strategy and operations as a key member of executive management
- Set up commercial insurance and workmen's compensation insurance for three domestic subs
- Add new assets and cars for insurance coverage
- Handle claims against insurance policies
- Oversee annual and midyear audit
- Negotiate audit fees
- Set tax strategy for company to minimize taxes
- Prepare annual Federal and State income tax returns
- Estimate and pay income taxes quarterly to appropriate agencies
- Assure optimum utilization of financial resources through sound forecasting and cash management

Qualifications:

- Good written and verbal communication skills
- Acquisitions and divestitures experience
- Financial systems integration experience
- Proficient with Microsoft Office Applications
- Degree = CPA and/or MBA
- Years of Experience = 15+ years financial experience
- 8-10 years in a managerial role
- Experience with manufacturing operations
- Excellent problem solving capability

Success Factor Snapshot

Chief Financial Officer

Success Factor 1: **Within twelve months, assess capital structure to support 15% per year growth targets.**

- Identify optimal equity/debt structure within ninety days. Hire a consultant within thirty days to provide industry data and assist in the analytical phase.
- Within six months, finalize planning and document a possible public/private equity offering to raise a minimum of $50M.
- Within twelve months, deliver a executable plan to achieve a $500 million valuation within five years.

Success Factor 2: **Develop the recommendation within twelve months to either keep/grow or divest/shutdown two under-performing business units.**

- Within three months, visit all locations, including sales, support, and manufacturing of the business units and conduct operational/strategic reviews with the management teams. Identify at least three major action items to improve manufacturing efficiency by 15%.
- Within six months, conduct an assessment of internal performance objectives for the business units against industry benchmarks, including visits to key customers, suppliers, and competitors in the industries served. Present the assessment to the board with specific recommendations to exceed industry averages by 10%.
- Within twelve months, create specific plans of action for the Board of Directors to move in either direction of keep/grow or divest/shutdown the two underperforming businesses.

Success Factor 3: **Reduce costs by 10% across-the-board to achieve EBIT objectives for the next fiscal year.**

- Establish cross-functional cost-reduction teams within three months. Teams will coordinate and manage all cost-reduction programs, completing work within 12 months.
- Within nine months, convince the seven key suppliers providing 80% of raw material and purchased sub-components to accept a 15% price reduction. Develop a back-up plan of alternative sourcing to ensure cost reduction targets of $700,000 within the first year.

The Heart And Soul Of Leadership

We firmly believe that the core of leadership in an organization is the ability—and willingness—to define key results and expectations in concrete, unambiguous terms, and then to leverage teams in order to achieve those goals.

We have seen enough failed executive hires that we firmly believe that **not defining Success at the individual level is an abdication of leadership.**

Chapter Summary

❖ **Hiring requires a project-management approach,** just as any other complex endeavor.

❖ **The Success Factor Methodology "projectizes" the hiring process.**

❖ **SOAR (Substantial departmental goal → Obstacles → Action → Results)** is a methodology that helps the hiring team to structure the definition of work for each position in specific, measurable terms.

❖ **Four steps produce the SFS:** 1) Assemble the hiring team and identity 3-4 substantial departmental goals. 2) For each substantial goal, define 2-3 Obstacles, Actions, and Results. 3) Consolidate *OARs* into individual Success Factors. 4) Compile Success Factors into the Success Factor Snapshot.

❖ **The heart and soul of leadership** is defining success at the individual level and linking that success to the organizational goals.

Chapter 7: How To Attract The Bottom Third Of Candidates

> Business is like a sports team; to win, you have to field the best talent.
>
> *Jack Welch*

The Best Candidates Don't Need The Job

As the candidate pyramid in Chapter 3 illustrated, the ideal candidates for most high-level, high-impact positions are *not* sitting at home reading want ads.

The Top 5% are generally already employed in jobs where they are happy (or at least comfortable). They have pensions building up. They're on a promotion track. Most Sleeper candidates have not even thought to look for another job in years, while Selective candidates may apply for an especially compelling opportunity.

Even if the best candidates are by some stroke of fate "between assignments," they often still do not *need* a job. Top candidates who are out of work tend to have an extraordinary network in place, get plenty of job offers (most of which they reject), and have plenty of jobs to choose from.

These are not people who are going to walk into the HR Department. You need to attract them through means beyond traditional want ads, arguing that your situation is a better opportunity than their current role or other roles they may be evaluating.

Regardless of these facts, we've discovered through our research that the sole strategy used by the majority of companies for sourcing candidates is: *Expose the open position through traditional want ads to those people who are actively seeking a new job.*

Never mind that people who are checking the job boards on a daily basis are not remotely close to the Top 5% of the candidate pool, let alone in the top third. In fact, most of these candidates are in the bottom third of the candidate pool. In over twenty years in our Executive Search Practice, we cannot recall the last time a Top 5% candidate was sourced through an advertisement or came from a posted resume on the job boards.

Let's take a look at how typical companies approach sourcing and why these efforts will frequently produce the bottom third of the candidate pool. (Again, we are not categorically saying that you can *never* find a good candidate using these methods, or that the methods themselves are particularly bad. It is just that they produce a shallow search that *feels* deceptively deep).

The Top Five Worst Sourcing Strategies

> 5. Run an ad in the local newspaper or an online job site
> 4. Use an outplacement firm
> 3. Ask friends and family for recommendations
> 2. Hope for a good walk-in applicant
> *1. No strategy at all*

The biggest problem with the first four approaches is that, while companies may think they're looking at four different candidate channels, they are usually just reaching the same people in four different ways.

It's much like fishing (badly) in a small pond. You've cast out several lines, but you haven't attached sinkers. So, rather than plumbing the depths, all your lines are simply floating along the top, skimming the surface of the pool. To make things even more difficult, there are lots of other people out there doing the same thing. Meanwhile, nobody's noticed the other ponds a few yards away.

Specifically, here's why we ranked the above methods as the top five *worst* sourcing channels.

Running A Traditional Ad. Whether it's placed in a newspaper, an online job board or with an organization you are affiliated with, a traditional ad is rarely going to reach the Selective and Sleeper Candidates you want to find.

Outplacement Firms. Outplacement firms facilitate job searches for people who have been laid off from other companies. These firms generally produce a large overlap with those who are reading ads.

Friends and Family. No offense intended; we're sure you love your family and trust your friends. But golfing buddies, yacht club members, country club compatriots, and in-laws don't (usually) know what your company needs to grow and thrive. While "asking around" may net you plenty of "friend of a friend" candidates, you shouldn't expect to find your Top 5% candidate this way. You need to go deeper.

Walk-Ins. Some candidates looking for a position will send resumes to companies for whom they'd like to work. While they're not *always* unemployed with good reason (or otherwise actively looking), these candidates tend to float near the top of the same pool as the other sources.

No Strategy at All. Speaks for itself.

The Wide World Of Traditional Sourcing

Let's look more specifically at the range of sourcing options available to find that Top 5% candidate. While this book specifically applies the Success Factor Methodology to executive and managerial hires, the same principles can be used effectively with all levels of staff. So it's worth reviewing typical candidate sourcing channels—even the ones that are more likely to net your next Administrative Assistant than the next Director of Administrative Services.

Walk-In Applicants	People who actually come to your place of business; increasingly rare channel, even for unskilled labor.
Employee Referrals	Usually involves some type of reward system; depending on the referrer. Should be a fantastic source, but usually is not.
Offline Advertising	Whether they're in print in the local newspaper or trade journal, or even broadcast on a local radio station, these generally reach folks who are looking for them. Job search trends indicate that the vast majority of candidates over the last few years are beginning to use online advertising as their preferred medium as opposed to offline advertising. Coinciding with this trend is the fact that home computer usage and internet access has surpassed cable TV penetration.
Online Advertising	Currently more than 85% of recruiters, including both third party recruiters and in-house corporate recruiters, are using the Internet to post jobs as their primary sourcing strategy (*source:* HR.com). No search is complete without this sourcing strategy; however, research we've conducted shows that less than 1% of high level positions are filled via online job boards and even at lower levels, online job board advertising generates between 10-15% of hired candidates (keep in mind these are "hires" not necessarily Top 5% candidates).

Searching On-Line Databases	Many of the major job boards have databases where Aggressive candidates have posted their resumes, hoping a company or recruiter will find them. Statistics quoted by the job boards and our research in this area shows a 25-to-1 ratio at best for candidates that respond to ads vs. those who post their resume. The database access fees are prohibitively expensive compared to the cost of posting an ad. Given the 25-to-1 ratio, companies will reap a higher ROI from posting nontraditional ads (we'll explore this in just a moment).
The Company Web Site	Valuable for finding Aggressive internal and external candidates who can apply online. Unfortunately, most company Web sites are a turn-off for Top 5% candidates. They are not candidate-oriented. Little is done to paint a compelling picture of the company and why people love working there.
Outplacement Services	Useful for networking; most likely to find unemployed (or soon-to-be unemployed) individuals. As mentioned before, this sourcing channel duplicates the effort of the other channels focusing on Aggressive Candidates.
College Campuses	For entry-level positions, placement offices and on-campus job fairs still can't be beat. Few companies use these to their full advantage.

Alumni Associations	Offer placement services and career counseling for new grads, and even better, stay connected to alumni as their careers develop.
Religious and Civic Organizations	Personal networking where the people doing the referring are trusted and are typically at a comparable career level.
Direct Mail Solicitation	Works best with focused target groups; scattershot approach is rarely successful.
Job Fairs	Usually hosted by a community in conjunction with several companies who set up a booth and entice entrants with information about benefits, etc. Again, the focus is on Aggressive Candidates.
Employment Agencies	Always ready and waiting to help to provide part-time, full-time temporary help and/or permanent placements at lower levels. Most are focusing on Aggressive Candidates. Most companies (using the methods we describe in this chapter) can source these same candidates for a few hundred dollars vs. thousands of dollars.
Networking	Industry associations remain a good source for spreading the word within your field. Unfortunately, the level of active executive networking usually occurs when an executive is unemployed, thereby yielding superficial referrals.
State Employment Services	"Your tax dollars at work…"

Contingency Recruiters	Provide multiple resumes to employers, hoping one of their candidates is hired. Only get paid if their candidate is hired. Typically, contingency recruiters look in their database and make a few phone calls in the attempt to pick some low-hanging fruit for a quick placement. Companies frequently spend thousands of dollars with contingency firms sourcing the same candidates they could have gotten off a compelling ad.
Retained Recruiters	Provide a dedicated search based on a contract, usually used for higher-level searches. Retained recruiters will frequently execute against a broad range of sourcing strategies and will invest heavily in the more lucrative channels of Top 5% candidates—particularly the Sleeper candidates.

Sounds like a lot of sources, doesn't it? And it is. A successful search for a key hire requires a broad-based approach, incorporating numerous concurrent strategies, to sourcing the candidate.

Executive and management hires based on the Success Factor Snapshots can be found in both traditional and nontraditional ways.

Building An Effective Sourcing Plan

To find that ideal candidate, you must create a sourcing plan that is specific to your needs and explores new avenues for finding that Top 5% Talent.

1. Begin with a compelling statement that focuses on the motivations of Top 5% candidates.
2. The Success Factor Snapshot will dictate the search strategy and sourcing channels you'll use to find a Top 5% candidate.
3. Once the sourcing channels have been identified, decide how to leverage the Compelling Marketing Statement.

Rule #1: Describe The Opportunity They Want, Not Your Needs

You don't need a graduate-level course in copywriting to put together a Compelling Marketing Statement. Snaring the Top 5% simply requires a touch of perspective, the ability to think like a Top 5% candidate, and a laser-like focus on our version of the Golden Rule: **Do Unto Candidates As You Would Have Employers Do Unto You.**

Most job advertising is about as inspiring as the list of ingredients on a mouthwash bottle. After reading four job ads in a row, eyes start to glaze over. "Five years of progressively responsible experience…" "Advanced knowledge of X software" "…solid background in A, B, and C methodologies…" A specific degree. A specific GPA. A specific salary range.

Zzzzzzzzzzzz.

We call this "the Drill Sergeant Approach" because it barks orders, usually in a tough-guy voice. Such ads are demanding and often borderline insulting, with no consideration of individual motivations and no understanding of "What's in it for them."

Drill Sergeant ads throw up as many roadblocks as they can to break down candidates' morale. They list a set of qualifications that often border on the ridiculous to "wash out" recruits.

Our experience is that this approach is almost guaranteed to attract the bottom 1/3 of the candidate pool. Such statements of work draw almost exclusively from the Aggressive candidate pool. And it's no wonder. Aggressive candidates who are actively looking for a new position are the only ones who would be willing to put up with the Drill Sergeant mentality—cold, impersonal, harsh demands.

Top 5% Talent, on the other hand, is turned off by this approach and runs in the other direction.

If you want to get the attention of candidates who *don't need your job*, you can't be a drill sergeant. Top Talent doesn't care what you want as an employer—they want to know, "What's in it for me?"

They don't need to jump through hoops. They're motivated by more than the need to pay the mortgage. They *want their career dreams and wishes fulfilled.*

Drill Sergeant Approach	Compelling Marketing Statement Approach
• Barks orders	• Whispers exclusive invitation
• All "head"	• All "heart"
• Just the facts	• Gets to feelings, dreams, ambitions, passions
• Demanding, intimidating, distancing, off-putting	• Inviting, warm, inclusive, enticing
• All about THE COMPANY	• All about THE CANDIDATE
• Exhaustive laundry list of To-Do's	• Comprehensive vision of success and achievement
• Thankless	• Grateful
• Mechanical	• Emotional
• Most likely to attract Aggressive candidates	• Most likely to attract Selective and Sleeper candidates
• Dismissive	• Respectful

One of the following examples is a drill sergeant approach and the other is a compelling marketing statement. Which one is more likely to attract the attention of a Top 5% Talent?

The Drill Sergeant Approach

We are a privately held owner/manager/developer of commercial real estate properties. Through our recent growth, we are seeking a candidate for a newly created position of Assistant Controller.

The ideal candidate will possess the following qualifications:
- 3 to 5 years commercial real estate accounting experience
- Track record of progressive growth in professional responsibilities
- Energetic self-starter with take-charge personality
- Experience with XXXYY Software
- Prior experience with XXXY billing and lease abstracting
- Ability to adapt, lead, and grow in ever-changing environment
- IT and computer system management experience
- CPA preferred

The responsibilities of the position include:
- Oversee daily accounting function of multiple entities
- Schedule and complete month-end closings
- Interface and communicate with out-of-state regional offices
- Assist in year-end tax package preparation
- Perform cash management functions
- Budgeting and cash projections
- Streamline accounting procedures for a multiple office operation
- Supervise staff of four

This position requires the following:
- BS/BA in Accounting or Finance from an accredited university
- Minimum 2 years experience in commercial real estate management accounting
- Ability to lead and communicate effectively

If you do not meet the requirements of the position, please do not apply. Principals only. This position is for local candidates only. No relocation assistance is available.

The position is based in our Boise offices and will offer a starting salary of $50,000 to $60,000 per annum depending on qualifications. Company paid benefits, and excellent potential for growth.

When You Wish Upon A Star: A Compelling Marketing Statement

Donald Trump knows real estate; are you his equivalent in Accounting?

We are seeking a very special person to: Be The Apprentice-Assistant Controller.

The right person for the job will grasp the issues of Real Estate Investor Trust (REIT) accounting and reporting, be able to communicate complex issues, enjoy the challenge of dealing with investors, and be willing to roll up their sleeves to make a measurable impact on the business.

If you...

- Are a businessperson first, with great ideas and creativity
- Understand the real estate business and how accounting can make an impact to help build a business
- Are looking for the excitement of real estate, the action of dealing with REITs, and the fun a growing company
- Are in a great job, but would like to jump-start your career
- Enjoy your work, but would really like to make a difference with your knowledge of real estate
- Are happy, but with the right opportunity could be happier
- Want more excitement, challenges, and reward for your efforts
- Want to be a part of a dynamic team

...then you might be the person our client is looking for! In this position, you will have a rare opportunity to be an active participant and work closely with the executive team, CFO, and investors. You must be "promotable" and be able to take on more responsibility. This job is about who you'll become versus who you've been.

Due to company growth and the investors' foray into new ventures, you'll be given the opportunity to demonstrate your knowledge and infuse your expertise as it relates to REITs that are publicly traded and include international investors.

This job is not about putting in time; it's about savvy business sense and leadership. The successful candidate will be career-driven, goal-oriented, passionate about their career, and committed to making a contribution to the team.

Our client believes in challenging their employees, because when people excel, the company benefits. And when the company benefits, the employees reap more rewards. It's a self-sustaining cycle of excellence, and it creates a culture that maximizes both work and fun.

Energize your career. Send us your resume, and start feeling great about what you do.

So, which of the two is more compelling?

The Drill Sergeant approach is focused on what the company wants. The ad's language isn't enticing. In fact, it's downright obnoxious. The only time it ever says the word "you" is to tell candidates that they must have all the requirements or they shouldn't bother to apply.

The Compelling Marketing Statement is all about the candidate. While it lists the requirements for the job, it does so in a way that makes the reader feel they are special and important. The writing is suggestive and inspirational—"you" "want" "opportunity" and "excitement." This is not a laundry list of orders—it is an invitation to exceptional people—an invitation to dream about a great new career prospect.

A few years ago, one of our partners was on a redeye flight from Los Angeles to Cleveland, seated next to an RN from a trauma center in Los Angeles. Being an executive recruiter, our partner couldn't resist: He asked what she did for a living, and why she liked it. The nurse launched into a twenty-minute oratory about how wonderful her job was, how amazing the people were, and how much she enjoyed working there. Finally, she paused, leaving room for one more question: "Tell me—how often do you venture online and check out the job boards just to see if there is a better opportunity for you out there?"

Without missing a beat, she said, "For the past year, once a week, I come home from my nursing shift on Friday afternoons, log on, and go to the Nursing job boards."

Our partner was stunned but curious. "If you've been doing this for a year, haven't you come across something interesting?"

She simply replied, "Almost every job sounds like the job I already have. I've already got a good job. Why would I want the same job somewhere else? There was one, but it was really way outside of the box. The heading for the job announcement didn't say RN or Nurse or Trauma Center Professional. It said, 'Do You Thrive on Chaos?'"

Her eyes lit up. That header had spoken directly to her. It got right to the heart of why she enjoyed working in a trauma center.

Ever since this encounter, our executive search firm has been carefully crafting compelling marketing statements to appeal to the ideal candidate's deepest motivations. We have been teaching our clients how to do this in our workshops and consulting engagements. Most have experienced a dramatic increase in the quantity and quality of great candidates.

Four Steps To A Compelling Marketing Statement

There are four key components to writing an effective Compelling Marketing Statement:
  1. The Headline
  2. The Challenge
  3. The Vision
  4. The Success Factors

The Headline

Entry-level copywriters on Madison Avenue learn that the most important part of writing effective copy is the headline—you must break through all the clutter and smack potential readers with a figurative brick between the eyes. Yet most job advertising, whether it be in the newspaper, online, or direct networking, is still using the *same* boring, mundane, out-of-date job titles/headlines that have been used since the beginning of time.

To grab a Top 5% candidate's attention, shake things up a bit.

Instead of HR Manager, ask for a **Chief Talent Officer**
Instead of Plant Manager, ask for a **Operation Fix-it Expert**
Instead of Sales Manager, ask for a **Olympic Sales Coach**
Instead of Quality Director, ask for a **Quality Maestro**

Another tactic to spice up your headline is to ask an intriguing question. Our partner's seatmate, the RN, got excited about "Do You Thrive on Chaos?" Perhaps a new Controller might respond to, "Enjoy Helping A Business Hit Its Profit Targets?" A Marketing Executive would stop for, "Constrained By A Non-Existent New Product Development Pipeline?"

Another tactic is to allude to current news, music, pop culture, events, or movies. The "Olympic Sales Coach" headline attracted a great number of Top Talented sales managers for a client in the middle of the 2002 Winter Olympics. Another client had great success with a movie reference. They had been searching for a technical stock trading expert for some time, running ad after ad with titles encompassing financial analysis, stock trading, stock analysis, etc.

We suggested they change the headline to: "Do You Have A Beautiful Mind?" (This advertisement appeared smack-dab in the middle of the film's popularity). At that point every math, statistics, and probability guru in a four-state region raised their hand to show their interest.

The Challenge

The second component of a Compelling Marketing Statement is "The Challenge," usually summed up in the first one or two sentences.

The challenge should be crafted in a way that gets right at the heart of why someone might be open to a better opportunity. For a CFO role, it might read, "Tired of being relegated to nothing more than a back-office function?" For a Product Design Director, we have used, "Frustrated by the lack of tools to do your job well?"

What are the specific frustrations, pains, or aggravations Top 5% Talent might currently be experiencing that your role can overcome? Figure them out and use them to get your best prospects nodding in agreement.

The Vision

The Third component of a Compelling Marketing Statement is the vision for your business, and the role this new individual will play in helping the company achieve the vision.

Ideally, you will be able to sum up your vision for the entire business in two or three compact statements, and then identify one or two ways the new hire will help to achieve that vision.

Numerous studies on candidate behavior in the interview process indicate that understanding the vision and their role in it is one of the most critical decision factors for Top Talent.

The Success Factors

The Fourth component of a Compelling Marketing Statement is the top 2-3 Success Factors from the Success Factor Snapshot.

Top 5% Talent want to know what they are going to be held accountable for, what type of impact they're going to have on your company, and what that project/impact might mean for their personal career. Offer a brief insight in two or three lines. For a product-engineering director: "You'll develop two new products based on our proprietary RF design over the next 12 months. You'll be recognized among your peer group nationally for your creative engineering abilities in R&D."

Visit our Web site to download examples for a variety of positions.

Leveraging The Right Sourcing Channels

There are three ways to use the completed Compelling Marketing Statement in your search for Top 5% Talent.

Employee "Natural" Networks

First, you can leverage the power of your employees' natural networks through an effective employee referral program.

In outstanding organizations, the minimum percentage of new hires from employee referrals is around 50%. If you're really doing a great job in this area, the percentage might be as high as 75% to 85%.

Employees are your most viable sourcing channel for finding Top Talent. Your best people already know other great people.

Attach the Compelling Marketing Statement to an email cover note and send it to employees in the target workgroup, department, or entire company. Maybe you'll even send it to your suppliers, vendors, and customers. The note should simply open the door. "Dear X, I am attaching a compelling statement of work for a critical role in our organization. We would appreciate your passing this along to friends, associates, or acquaintances who you think might meet our high expectations and who would find this opportunity compelling. We're not just interested in those individuals who have told you they need a job—we're interested in talking with the best people you've worked with or know."

Online Job Boards

A second key sourcing target should be online job boards, simply because you need to make the position as visible as possible. One target should be a "big" board like Monster.com, Careerbuilder. com, or Hotjobs.com. But we also suggest placing the Compelling Marketing Statement on specialty sites that are unique to both the open functional role (such as project management, electronic design, semiconductor fab management) or industry sectors.

Leave an online job advertisement up for just two weeks at a time. If you have not yet pulled the right group of candidates within two weeks, take it down and completely rewrite it. Change the headline, challenge, and vision. Phrase things a little bit differently.

It sometimes takes three or four iterations of the Compelling Marketing Statement before you tap into the right motivations of candidates you're seeking to attract.

Candidate "Natural" Networks

A third key sourcing tactic is to disseminate the word to leverage other "natural" networks where potential candidates may reside.

Think along two dimensions for this sourcing strategy.

First, where do the candidates you desire to attract spend time with each other? What locations and places do they congregate to pursue professional, learning, educational, hobbies, and other interests?

Second, what groups do they belong to, either online or offline? Once you get the name of the group, you can identify the leaders or facilitators and email them a copy of the Compelling Marketing Statement. Generally, if you approach it this way (rather than spamming a group without permission), people are happy to spread the word.

Example: Calling All CFOs

Where do CFOs go, congregate, or hang out with each other?

CFO/Financial executive seminars and workshops
- Symposia hosted by investment bankers
- Morning breakfast sessions run by major banks

What groups do CFOs join?
- Local CFO roundtables
- Alumni associations of major business schools
- Financial Executive Networking Forum (FENG)
- Financial Executives Institute (FEI)
- Financial sub-groups of industry trade associations
- Local chapters of the AICPA

For most positions at an executive or managerial level, there are numerous venues and groups to tap into.

Leveraging the power of natural networks of potential candidates brings a tremendous degree of efficiency to the search process and frequently yields Top 5% Talent.

Using these three sourcing strategies along with your Compelling Marketing Statement should enable you to fill the bulk of your hiring needs quickly, easily, and efficiently. The key to success in using these sourcing strategies is to execute against all three of them concurrently. You'll rapidly discover which strategy is bearing the most fruit and be able to invest or refocus your energy in that direction.

Chapter Summary

❖ **Top 5% Talent does not need your job,** so they won't be reached through halfhearted and redundant sourcing.

❖ **Typical methods of looking for candidates are ineffective** because they only skim the surface of the market.

❖ **Write Compelling Marketing Statements that are about the candidate, not the company.** If you want to find the perfect candidate, speak to their dreams and wishes.

❖ **Build a more effective sourcing plan** by concurrently targeting your employees' natural networks, online advertising, and the candidate natural networks.

Chapter 8: What Color Is Your Petri Dish? Cultural Considerations and "Fit"

> It is critical that…new hires are a good fit with the current culture. If an individual is out of synch with the culture, the organization's cultural antibodies will often attack.
>
> *Hagberg Consulting Group*

Quick: What's Your Culture?

Work pace. Decision-making. Responsibility. Authority. Communication. Formality. Risk and reward structures.

Organizational culture encompasses a vast constellation of unspoken, undocumented norms, values, expectations, and behaviors. While some aspects may end up on the front page of the Web site under a heading that says "Mission Statement," most cultural attributes are never analyzed, identified, or codified.

Culture in most organizations is simply understood as "the way things get done around here." In large organizations, the culture is often deeply ingrained in every employee from the CEO on down, and it is highly resistant to change.

In other words, whatever your organizational culture is, people who join the company will need to adapt to it. It will not budge for them. A new hire must be able to feel comfortable in your organization's unique stew of politics, patterns, and pacing. If new employees cannot adapt, they will not be able to succeed—no matter how strong their prior accomplishments are.

103

Before we get into a discussion of the ways cultural mismatches can influence the success or failure of a new hire, you might want to take this quick self-test. Think about your company as you circle the closest match in each column.

Cultural Dimension	Circle The Closest Match To Your Company		
Dress Code	Suits and ties rule the day.	Polo shirts and khakis are *de rigueur.*	Shorts, flip-flops, and t-shirts are about the best you can expect most days.
How Management Communicates With Staff	Drowning in documentation (memos, emails, all-employee voicemails, etc.)	One-on-one conversations and staff meetings.	Staff depends on grapevine, water cooler, and guesswork.
Pace Of Work	Fast and furious.	Accuracy before speed.	Slow and steady wins the race.
Risk Tolerance	Risk-taking is rewarded and "skunk-works" are everywhere.	New initiatives and ideas must be OK'd by management first.	"It ain't broke. Don't fix it!"

Competition/ Cooperation	People here climb to the top…stepping all over each other.	Friendly competition keeps us sharp, but we all pitch in when the going's rough.	Nobody's ever too busy to lend somebody a helping hand.
Teams	A team is a group of people who exist to meet the needs of the leader.	Everyone has responsibilities in our teams, but it's a nonhierarchical structure.	We are Borg. You will be assimilated. Resistance is futile.
Affirmation/ Acknowledgment	Your reward for good work is that you get to keep your job.	There's an occasional "attaboy" for really noteworthy contributors.	It's so positive around here, this place seems like the *Brady Bunch*.
Emotional Atmosphere	Intensity is our middle name; the whole company needs Botox to erase our frown lines.	We strike a balance between goal orientation and having a good time.	We all love coming to work; it's like group therapy, only happier.
Working Hours	Everything is a crisis: We arrive at dawn and work until moonrise, seven days a week.	8:30 to 5:00 is normal, and if we need to work longer for "crunch time," it's an exception.	So long as you get the work done, "face time" isn't important.

Work/Life Balance	If you have a life elsewhere, that's your problem. We certainly didn't issue you one.	We want you to take care of yourself so others don't have to do your job when you're sick.	Happy, healthy workers make better, stronger companies. Onsite yoga, anyone?
Age Of Workforce	Most of our employees were born after Madonna hit the scene.	A wide range of ages and experience.	Gray is beautiful.
Ethics	Did it work? That's all that matters. Greed is good.	No secrets; we do what we have to do to stay competitive, but we are not afraid to be subpoenaed.	The Golden Rule and a strict code of ethics rule the day.
If the company were a movie character, it would be...	Gordon Gecko	Indiana Jones	Mary Poppins

Goal Timeframe Orientation	Short-term goals are everything; what are the numbers today? We have to get them up tomorrow.	Short-term goals and long-term goals are weighted equally.	The long haul and the grand vision drive the company; if we have to lose money for three quarters to achieve long-term goals, we will.

Those are just a few of the dimensions that make up what it is commonly referred to as "corporate culture." Hiring executives need to understand and be able to clearly communicate this culture to prospective candidates, because cultural mismatches account for a significant percentage of hiring mistakes.

It's critical to define the company culture in a succinct manner, because the hiring team needs to describe it in both the Compelling Marketing Statement and every interview with potential candidates.

Some candidates are naturally more flexible than others; they can work productively and happily in a number of different cultures and environments. Others require clear hierarchy, direction, and specific procedures and processes to flourish. "Creative" personalities may conversely need freedom to attack problems in their own unique way; nighthawks might succeed best if their workday runs from 10:00 am to 7:00 pm, rather than 8:00 am to 5:00 pm.

During the interview process, share honest, frank assessments of the company culture with candidates. There's no payoff in hiding the fact that employees are routinely expected to work 60+ hour weeks during "crunch time," or that people rarely leave the building on their lunch break. A candidate who will not fit in with the norms, behaviors, expectations, and common practices of your specific corporate culture will not stay, no matter how much you pay him or her. That's a simple fact.

In our experience, when there has been a gaping cultural mismatch between the candidate and the organization, a new hire will not succeed in the long term *even if* he or she can meet each and every Success Factor in your Snapshot.

Generally, the more rigid your corporate culture, the more difficult it will be for new hires to "fit" in. If your culture is a bit looser, you may find that two or three buttoned-down, business-school types can make a comfortable place for themselves within the organization (assuming they're given the freedom to do their own thing). But if your company always works at the speed of light with little top-down direction, the likelihood is small that a methodical, analytical, precise, by-the-books candidate will be able to succeed.

As you move into the interviewing stage of your search, be prepared to show candidates a true picture of the company, warts and all. It's cheaper and easier to uncover personality and cultural conflicts *before* a hire than *after*.

Chapter Summary

❖ **Corporate Culture** is one of the prime factors that will decide whether any given individual will be able to succeed in the company.

❖ **Awareness and the Ability** to specifically describe your culture is a prerequisite for a good cultural fit.

❖ **Honesty and up-front assessment** of your culture during the interview process is an absolute necessity.

❖ **Misrepresenting cultural "negatives"** to attract somebody through the front door will simply result in them leaving through the back door. Candidates must be given what they need to make an informed choice to join your organization.

SECTION 3: INTERVIEWING AND BEYOND

Chapter 9: Before The First Candidate Arrives

> It is better to look ahead and prepare than to look back and regret.
>
> *Jackie Joyner-Kersee*

Preparing for a round of Success Factor-based interviews is no small task. To hire Top 5% Talent, you must be properly equipped emotionally, mentally, and even physically.

Up-front preparation will enable you to avoid the most common pitfalls that allow under qualified candidates to slip through the cracks, while best matches slip away unrecognized.

Emotional Preparation

The interview process often brings out the worst in interviewers.

This isn't a matter of malice; as is the case with many other managerial skills, interviewing is rarely taught as a concrete skill. As a result, hiring executives do what they think they "ought" to do, follow common wisdom, interview like they were interviewed, and usually miss the target entirely.

The problem is that most interviews are geared toward elimination. From the moment a candidate arrives, the interviewer is scrutinizing, looking for reasons to reject the candidate. Clammy hands? Outta here! Scuffs on the shoes? Gone!

When hiring executives follow common wisdom (*"Look for the most enthusiastic, personable candidate"*), they aren't open to the full range of evidence. And they are at grave risk of missing the best candidate—one who may not be the most polished interviewer, but who *is* the best fit for the job.

Then there's the matter of "chemistry." We humans tend to form snap judgments—to decide we "like" or "dislike" people based on just a few seconds of interaction. Perhaps they have mannerisms and qualities that we appreciate—or that we find irritating. They may remind us of a favorite uncle, or a despised Ex. They may have the same accent as everybody from our hometown. Perhaps they remind us of a "younger version" of ourselves—full of promise and enthusiasm. Maybe they follow the same football team as the interviewer—or may not follow sports at all, which the interviewer finds unimaginable. Unfortunately, none of these things have anything to do with a person's ability to do the job.

First Impressions—And How To Minimize Their Impact

First impressions interfere with objectivity and distort the interviewing process.

The key to emotional preparation is to recognize the *power of first impressions* and take conscious steps to recognize and then minimize their effect on the overall interview.

Drawing a first impression is a natural human reaction. It is unavoidable. No matter how you prepare, you are going to react in an instant to superficial physical characteristics and personal mannerisms. Sometimes the first impression will be negative, sometimes positive. Regardless, the first impression rarely correlates with reality.

As professional recruiters and interviewers, we confess that we too still struggle with the power of a first impression—good or bad. However, as professionals, we've learned how to recognize and then minimize that effect. We've learned that focusing on what the candidate needs to accomplish and working through a structured interviewing methodology, we can achieve a very high level of objectivity in the assessment of talent.

Effective interviewers learn to tame their surface impressions. The following are several techniques that will force you to more objectively interview the different candidates.

Use The Phone First

A VP of HR we worked with told us once that if he had it his way, every interview would be done with blindfolds on. That's how strongly he felt that physical impressions interfered with objectivity and analysis.

While blindfolds may be a little too extreme, you can use the telephone to achieve nearly the same effect. Before you meet candidates face-to-face, conduct thorough pre-interview phone calls. Take at least thirty minutes to discuss one or two of your critical Success Factors. This will allow you to gather vital data about the candidate's successes and capabilities (first impressions you can actually use), without irrelevant and distracting physical attributes like what kind of suit, watch, or shoes the candidate has chosen to wear for the interview.

Phone pre-screens can give you a good idea of how candidates might perform in the job without distracters like a crooked tie. As a result, when you do meet the candidate, you will be able to conduct the in-person interview in a more objective frame of mind. (Visit our Web site to download our 30-minute Success Factor Phone Screen Script™.)

111

> Few have strength of reason to overrule the perceptions of sense, and yet fewer have curiosity or benevolence to struggle long against the first impression: he who therefore fails to please in his salutation and address is at once rejected, and never obtains an opportunity of showing his latest excellences or essential qualities.
>
> *Samuel Johnson*

Use The Same Structure For Every Interview

If you decide at the end of the phone interview to bring the candidate in for a physical face-to-face interview, you should send the candidate an abbreviated form of the Success Factor Snapshot and explain the type of interview you'll be conducting.

Once the candidates are in front of you and ready to talk, a structured interview will allow you to evaluate each candidate using the same yardstick. The importance of a uniform interviewing protocol cannot be overemphasized. If you are asking each candidate a different set of questions, there is no legitimate way to compare their qualifications and prospects for success.

It's common for untrained interviewers to ask candidates they like "softball" questions. There is a natural tendency to seek out information that confirms first impressions and to discard information that disagrees with them. Many hiring mistakes happen because hiring executives *want* to hire a particular person and look for confirming evidence.

Despite the fact that you may never choose to play golf or go out socially with the quiet, nervous candidate for your open accounting position, she may be the one who can meet every Success Factor.

And despite the fact that you and the next applicant are both alumni of the same obscure Midwestern public university and grew up in the same town, that's no excuse to let him skate through the interview.

If you have a good feeling early on about a particular candidate, *be tougher on yourself.* Are you sticking to the structured interview script? Are you challenging them as much as the one with the untied shoelaces? Are you digging deep into the candidate's background even though your gut says, "He's like a long-lost friend! He should work out great"?

If at any time during the interview you discover that you've strayed from the structured approach or other interview best practices, stop. Take a deep breath. Take a drink of water. Offer the candidate a glass of water. Anything that will help you to regroup and get back on track.

Take Your Time With Each Candidate

Give yourself time to form an opinion. You should at least wait until you have finished the first or second interview question before you decide you "like" or "dislike" a candidate.

Keep the finish line in sight. Use your Success Factor Snapshot to guide you through the interview. Stay the course. By the time you've finished interviewing your candidate, you will be well informed and capable of comparing him against all other candidates. Only then will one candidate begin to emerge as the best qualified and best adaptable for your organization.

In our years of combined executive search experience, we cannot find a single correlation between how well somebody interviews and their on-the-job success. However, interviewers often fixate on, and even base decisions on, irrelevant things that have little to do with success.

What are some of your subconscious biases? What do you tend to notice, maybe even fixate on? Think about this question before the first interview even begins, and try to come up with a list of the things that bother you during an interview. For instance:

- What is the one thing you can't stand for a candidate to do?
- What do you wish candidates would do? Why?
- Do you come into the interview process with preconceived ideas about how candidates should "act"?
- Do you only take notes when they say something that bothers you?
- Do you tend to let the interview take on a life of its own—having no direction or structure?
- Do you spend most of the interview time talking about the company or yourself, instead of the position and the candidate's accomplishments?
- Do you believe the best candidate is one who can withstand a few jabs or tricks from you?

To minimize unconscious bias as much as possible, create your own list of personal peeves. Do a few of these sound familiar?
- Dirty shoes
- Punctuality
- Hairstyle
- Weight
- Clothing
- Speech mannerisms
- Speed/jitters/"energy"
- Regional or ethnic accents
- "Performance under pressure" (may not be relevant to job!)
- Posture
- Eye contact
- Handshake
- Vocal tone
- Articulation
- Attractiveness

We make it a point to tell our executive clients that they need to be more sensitive to the stress and pressures that can interfere with a candidate's ability to be "all they can be" during an interview.

Do you remember the last interview you went on? Did you have to drive in rush hour traffic to get there on time? Did you give up a vacation day with your family? How were you treated when you arrived? Were you kept waiting? Were you on a timed schedule and needed to get done and back to the office? How did you feel just before you went in and during the process?

Most people experience some level of anxiety regarding being interviewed. An interview is not familiar territory for most people, including Top Talent (who do not routinely beat the bushes for work). Interviews are unnatural situations, which is why we caution the interviewer to remember that many physical factors are well beyond a person's control.

Under stress, the body's natural reactions (called the General Adaptation Syndrome) include increased heart rate, breathing and perspiration. Their stomach clenches; they ramble; they shift in their seat. These are all physiological responses to stress and adrenaline. They are not automatic reasons to disqualify a candidate from consideration—unless the candidate is being interviewed for a Crisis Communications position in the PR Department.

Anyone who has been pulled over by a highway patrolman has experienced that flustered sensation as they try to find their license and registration and can't seem to find anything; most job candidates, regardless of their qualifications, are feeling the same thing.

So, despite common wisdom that's been floating around for eons, does a clammy handshake really tell you if a person will be a good line manager? Not likely.

If a person doesn't maintain eye contact, should you exclude them? No way, especially with today's diverse employee base.

And what if the candidate seems too quiet or shy during the interview? Does that mean they won't fit in? Probably not—especially if you did all the talking or came across extremely strong during the interview.

Reliable assessments are not based on superficial, irrelevant factors. Extrapolations based on these factors too often end up eliminating outstanding candidates because first impressions biased the interview and distracted the hiring team from the candidate's track record of success.

The common wisdom about interviewing is that it's up to the candidates to prove they can do the job. The hiring executive, by contrast, sits back and waits to be blown away. That's a recipe for disaster. It's the hiring team's responsibility to extract the necessary information from the candidate to determine if they can be successful in the position.

A Word To The Wise

Cut 'em some slack.

Create an environment that allows the candidate to relax and get down to the task of showing you why she's the best choice for the job.

Once you take the time to build a little rapport and help her get into her groove—she'll show you what she's made of and how her talent, education, adaptability, past, and current performance have made a difference and relate to what you need accomplished.

Process Preparation

Once you are emotionally prepared and mentally determined to keep an open mind throughout the first round of interviews, it's time to prepare the specific interview team and create questions that will guide your objective review of the candidates.

The First Interview

For the first interview, the hiring manager or human resources director will most likely go one-on-one with candidates. That person will generally determine whom to invite back for the next round of deeper interviews.

During the first interview, simply be sure to hit the high points of the Success Factor Snapshot you wrote for the open position. You're trying to determine whether or not this candidate has actually done some of the things you need accomplished. Based on their responses, you can then make a comparison to other candidates and determine whom you want to invite back for the next round of interviews.

Second And Subsequent Interviews

A typical interview process for executive or senior management candidates might involve four to five interview sessions. These will typically include additional one-on-one time with the hiring executive and other members of the interviewing committee.

An efficient strategy is to combine other members on the interview committee into panel interviews with no more than three or four people (anything more takes on an atmosphere of an interrogation). Panel interviews are more efficient for the candidates as well. They need only spend 90 minutes with the panel, rather than four hours hopping from office to office repeating themselves.

Panels ensure that evaluations are more objective. Having several interviewers in the room at once helps to eliminate the subconscious biases of one person, because there will be enough separate observers to balance out any misleading first impressions.

Finally, the panel format offers a chance to put candidates "in the job." Since most top-level positions will require extensive group presentations and the ability to communicate effectively in the boardroom, the panel interview helps to assess such skills firsthand. (Of course, some candidates will be more nervous than others, but even so, a candidate with the ability to communicate effectively and persuasively in a group setting will be able to demonstrate this skill in a panel interview.)

So, who should sit on the interviewing panel? Take a look back to the Success Factor Snapshot and ask yourself these questions:

- Which departments or managers are closely related to this position and how will this person affect them?
- Who will the candidate be working with, initially and in the future?
- Who understands expectations of the position?
- Who reports directly to the person in the position?
- To whom does the position report?

You should select three or four people for each interview (there may be several) who will be able to intelligently ask relevant questions that explore the candidate's ability to succeed in the position based on the SFS.

It is critical that the interview team be prepared up front for their role and briefed on what to do—and what not to do. Panel interviews should be *discussions*, not cross-examinations, so set up a round-table atmosphere. When panel members focus their questions around the obstacles identified in the Success Factor Snapshot, an interview can become a simulated problem-solving session, much like a staff meeting.

High-level executive and managerial hires typically require up to twenty hours of interaction with the top candidates. Midlevel hires can take half as much time. Regardless of how many interviews there are or how many people are on each panel, the full Success Factor Snapshot must be covered before you can call the process "finished."

Each follow-up interview needs to be prepared for as extensively as the first, and each member of the team needs to be briefed on the necessity to focus on the job, not personality or physical factors.

Follow-up interviews are the place to probe deeper into areas of potential concern that were raised after earlier sessions. For example, if the candidate spent most of the second interview speaking exclusively in the first-person singular ("*I* did this; *I* accomplished that; *I* designed X; *I* implemented Y"), and your organization is strongly team-focused, a third interview should focus on the candidate's past accomplishments in teambuilding.

Though it is important to use the same questions for the first round of interviews to eliminate subconscious preferences and bias, follow-up interviews will be highly individualized. Interview panel preparation should involve assigning various Success Factor questions to different members of the panel, ensuring that panel members have specific and useful questions to ask, and deciding what homework to assign for the final candidates.

Environmental Preparation

The hiring process is like courtship; you are trying to woo these candidates. Just as hiring executives form first impressions, so do candidates. Through the years, we have occasionally been genuinely shocked at how some companies treat job candidates. One of them will become a valued asset, potentially responsible for millions of dollars in sales, profit, people, and clients.

Every candidate deserves to be treated as the significant investment she potentially is: You should commit here and now to treating potential hires as you would treat your top customer, from the moment they walk through the door.

You need to evaluate your company's physical and environmental factors that candidates will be exposed to before, during and after the interview.

- How are they greeted and by whom?
- Where are they asked to wait?
- For how long are they left waiting?
- Do you treat them like honored guests?
- Do you thank them for their time and effort?
- Does the interview process say "We want you," or "Don't call us—we'll call you"?

These things make a major difference in hiring Top 5% Talent. When you treat a candidate as if he or she were a $10 million customer, they naturally relax and perform better in their interview. Plus, they will be far more interested in coming to work for your company and contributing to an organization that deserves their talents.

Every candidate who walks through your doors either goes back to tell friends and colleagues what an awful experience it was, or becomes an advocate for your firm.

Whether or not the interview experience was pleasant or not is completely within your control—not hers.

Don't Do This

One company we worked with several years ago was having a major problem getting top candidates to come back for follow-up interviews. As a part of our work with the organization, we asked candidates being interviewed to fill out an assessment of their experience.

Nearly every candidate remarked they didn't like the room where they were sent to wait for the interview to begin, and that they had been made to wait too long.

It turned out that the company had been ushering candidates into a small, claustrophobic, gray room. There were no windows or décor—just a gray table and four chairs. No reading material, no artwork, poor lighting—you get the idea.

Candidates were kept waiting, on average, for fifteen minutes in this room. By the time they were escorted to the office of the interviewer, they felt like they were in a police interrogation, not a company that would value their talents.

Based on recommendations we made, the company painted the walls a bright, cheerful color, added art to the walls, and replaced the gray furniture with upholstered pieces that were far more inviting. They laid out glossy magazines and industry publications, added a tabletop lamp with a warm incandescent bulb, and made the space far more inviting and comfortable—just like the rest of their offices. They also committed to beginning interviews within five minutes of a candidate's scheduled appointment.

These simple physical changes made an enormous impression. The candidates they really wanted were more than happy to come back and pursue opportunities, and all it took was a bit of attention to physical space and reception details.

Another client company who was searching for a high-level executive *refused to validate parking* for the candidates. In Los Angeles, that meant it cost candidates $20 per interview day to apply for the job. Our philosophy is quite simple: If you are prepared to spend $90,000 a year on a person's salary, you should be *happy* to invest $200 in parking to get the right candidate.

Occasionally, we speak with an executive who wants to "weed out" candidates who do not send thank-you notes promptly after each interview. While we understand this age-old part of the hiring courtship dance, we counter by asking these executives whether they have sent a thank-you card or email to each of the candidates.

"What? Why should *I* send a thank-you note to the *candidates*?"

Because the candidates are the ones who have invested the time and energy to offer their skills and ability to succeed, with no promise of a payoff.

Because they've driven through town, sometimes during rush hour, or even flown halfway across the country to meet you.

Because they've taken hours out of their current job (usually involving a significant bit of uncomfortable deception) to spend time discussing your problems and your needs, and sometimes offering the seeds of a solution—for free.

Because they are often considering uprooting their family to come help you and your organization.

Because it's the right thing to do.

Finally, because when they get a "Thank You" note from you, their jaw will hit the floor. That one simple gesture increases the likelihood that the candidate you really want will be willing to accept your offer when it comes to that point.

The bottom line is, candidates should enjoy the interview process as much as possible from the moment they arrive. Isn't it true that you're interviewing to find that needle in the haystack? Well, it's also true that candidates are looking for the exception to the rule.

Differentiate your firm from all others. If you want to attract the best, you too have to be the best.

Are You Prepared?

- Your receptionist should be briefed on how to speak to candidates and where to direct them.

- Your lobby or waiting area should be comfortable and appealing.
- Do not make a candidate wait for an extended amount of time. If there is a delay, be sure the candidate is checked on or offered refreshment.
- Set aside an interview space that is private, yet inviting. Do not allow interruptions or phone calls during the interview.
- After the interview, walk them to the door and be sure to say "Thank you!"

Each of these things is simple, but makes a major difference in how your company is perceived. Make sure they feel respected and know that you appreciate that they took time out of their busy schedule to meet with you.

Chapter Summary

❖ **Before the candidates arrive**, you and your hiring team must prepare in three critical areas: Emotions, Processes, and Environment.

❖ **Emotional Preparation** requires being aware that first impressions are powerful, natural, and recognition is the key to minimizing their impact.

❖ **Process Preparation** requires assembling an interview team and ensuring that every member of the team understands 1) their role in the interview, 2) what is being measured, and 3) the questions they'll be asking.

❖ **Environmental Preparation** requires putting the "best face" on your company in order to attract the Top 5%. You're not doing candidates a favor; one of them will soon have the responsibility and authority to make or break a critical department. Treat them *all* accordingly.

Chapter 10: Face-To-Face Interviews That Aren't A Waste Of Time

> Take nothing on its looks; take everything on evidence. There's no better rule.
>
> *Charles Dickens, Great Expectations*

The sole purpose of an employment interview is to investigate whether the candidate can succeed in the open position.

Read that statement one more time, aloud. It's important.

Even in enormous multinational companies, it's common for interviewing, like other non-core business practices, to be handled "on the fly." Without a clear interview structure, both interviewer and candidate tend to flounder, meander and ramble. "Time-honored" interview questions elicit time-honored responses: ("My weaknesses? Well, sometimes I tend to be a perfectionist. Oh, and I've been told I work too hard.")

There are dozens of books with hundreds of interview questions that you can type up and then claim you use a structured interview process. You may ask 1,000 questions in a long series of interviews. But, if they're the wrong questions, you aren't going to know any more at the end of the interview than you did at the beginning.

Troubleshooting The Typical Interview

The problem with most interviews is that they never get to the core issue: *Can this candidate succeed in the open position?*

Instead, most interviews skip along the surface of a candidate's resume at 40,000 feet, pausing here or there for an anecdote, or for a brief "Tell me more."

Alternatively, they turn into interrogations—hostile encounters where the interviewer sprays the candidate with rapid-fire accusatory questions, seemingly convinced at the outset that every line on the resume is an embellishment or an outright lie.

Neither interview style is likely to result in hiring the best candidate for the job. Fact is, most common interview questions ask for the same generic information, over and over and over. Interviewers hope some of them will help to uncover critical "culture" and "fit" issues, but they don't. Candidates hope they can respond to the questions in a way that tells the interviewer what they want to hear.

Useless Interview Questions

- Tell me about yourself.
- What are your strengths?
- What are your weaknesses?
- Why do you want to work here?
- Why did you leave your last job?
- Why should I hire you?
- How do you feel about _____?
- Where do you see yourself in five to ten years?
- What can you do for us that another person can't?
- If you were an animal/tree/plant, what would you be?
- How do you feel about long working hours?

The problem with each of these questions is that that they do not focus on what's needed to get the job done. They aren't relevant to the position's Success Factors. They don't allow an interviewer to ascertain, "Will this candidate succeed at what needs to be done?"

A systematic, structured interview based around the Success Factor Snapshot is critical to hiring successful, Top 5% performers.

Before The Questions: Building Rapport

In our years as executive recruiters, we've seen interviewers stumble occasionally in the first few minutes of an interview. When you are conducting a Success Factor-based interview, it's vital to create conditions that make candidates feel comfortable sharing in-depth information about their background, including their current position.

Candidates need to feel safe about discussing situations and experiences that may be sensitive. So, before diving into the "meat and potatoes" of the interview, take five to seven minutes to establish an appropriate mood and tone for what's ahead.

Break The Ice

Basic "small talk" can go a long way toward relaxing candidates enough to ensure a fair interview.

> *"Thank you for coming in today. How was your drive?"*
>
> *"Did you have any trouble finding the office?"*
>
> *"Can I get you something to sip…water or coffee?"*
>
> *"Can I take your coat/jacket?"*

While it may seem unnecessary to mention these basic courtesies, it's not unusual for hiring executives to skip right over them in their zeal to get to the heart of the matter. A comfortable candidate is a more honest, candid candidate.

Set The Stage

Next, describe the type of interview you're about to conduct.

> *"We're going to spend about an hour together in a Success-Factor based discussion. I'm going share with you the critical success factors we need accomplished over the next 12-18 months. I'll ask you to give me two or three examples for each critical Success Factor of comparable achievements, accomplishments, results, deliverables, outcomes, and success from your past. I'd like you to answer in as much detail as you feel comfortable sharing. Occasionally I'll ask you to go into more depth*

*about your past successes, or to give me a concrete example or illustration.
We'll also discuss how you would achieve the Success Factors in our
organization if you got the job."*

Obviously, it's best if the interview format isn't "sprung" on the
candidate on the day of the first face-to-face. They should already
have been briefed on this structure ahead of time, during phone
screenings and the invitation to be interviewed. Your "setting the
stage" is just a way of easing into a form of interview that will in all
likelihood be foreign to many candidates.

Most candidates are expecting the interview to be just like every
other interview they've ever been through (or even like the ones
they conduct) in which the interviewer regurgitates the resume, line
by line, occasionally pausing to ask the useless questions like those
listed above. When unprepared candidates encounter questions
about accomplishments, achievements, outcomes, and results,
they may freeze like a deer caught in oncoming headlights. That's
why "setting the stage" is a critical element of having a successful
interview.

Three other key items to share with the candidate before you start
asking questions:

- **Make the job important.** You should stress the opportunity
  and importance of the open position. It's a basic law of
  human nature that people like to feel important. Make the
  candidate understand up front how the job is a critical part
  of the company's overall future success. We suggest in our
  workshops that you should literally take the job and put it up
  on a pedestal. Here's a typical statement:

  *"This Vice President of Operations role is absolutely critical to our
  future success. Unless we can improve our on-time deliveries, lower our
  cost of manufacturing substantially, and service our key customer base,
  which is now shifting from North American to the Asia, we will not*

be competitive in a three-to-five year timeframe. That's why we are focusing on this role as one of the linchpins of our future success."

You can frame up any executive or managerial hire in a similar format.

- **State two or three of the most critical Success Factors up front.** This serves as a preview for the candidate and helps to get him or her thinking about comparable situations, accomplishments, examples, and anecdotes.

- **Share the vision for your company two to three years from now.** Without burning up too much time, share with the candidate the compelling vision of the future for your business. In addition, demonstrate how this role will specifically impact that vision. You've already developed the vision during the writing of the Compelling Marketing Statement—now all you have to do is get everyone on the interview committee to be able to share the same picture.

Some additional thoughts to keep in mind as you conduct the interview:

- **Listen more than you talk.** There are various ratios floating around out there: 80/20, 70/30, 75/25. The underlying message is the same. You need to spend the bulk of your time *listening* to what the candidate says and probing for deeper understanding.

  Don't drown them with information about ACME Widgets. Interview time is too valuable not to hear as much as you can from each person you speak to.

- **Give them enough time to respond.** A companion guideline is that you should expect to cover only two to three Success Factors, in depth, per interview hour. It takes approximately twenty minutes to uncover enough information per example to validate the truth.

- **Get beyond the resume.** As quickly as possible, put down the candidate's resume and return focus to the Success Factor Snapshot. You're looking for information that will never emerge from a resume, so don't lean on that summary document for anything other than a stripped-down chronology of where and when the candidate has worked. We're not saying the resume isn't valuable, but let others in your organization, perhaps HR, focus on why someone left their last position, or why they chose a certain career path, or where they see themselves in five years. Focus on the individual—the flesh and blood sitting in front of you. Ask and you shall receive the information you want and need.

- **Take notes on what they are saying rather than planning your next question.** You need to record what candidates say as they say it. Don't count on memory alone to guide you through the evaluation process later; take notes as candidates answer, and make them extensive. This also sends a message to the candidate that you're serious about this process and they'll know you're engaged in it. Take the same depth of notes for every candidate you meet.

- **If the interview session is going to span the lunch hour, take them to lunch.** Another basic social detail, but we've seen hiring executives send a candidate away for an hour, asking them to return after lunch. Even worse, we've seen hiring executives continue to grill through the lunch hour, to the point where the candidate's stomach growls louder than the air-conditioning kicking on and off. Because one of these candidates is going to end up responsible for the heart and soul of a department, isn't the next CFO or Director of Security worth lunch at a family restaurant chain—or even a steakhouse? Pair her up with another peer-level employee and send them off to get to know each other.

The "Five Key Question" Interview

Through our work in the past twenty years with Top 5% Talent and the companies that hire them, we have identified five keys that are universal predictors of success.

The first three predictors focus on the longstanding patterns of Top 5% candidate behavior, and the final two are designed to test the candidate's ability to achieve the Success Factor Snapshot within your organization.

- High initiative
- Flawless execution
- Leadership
- Comparable Success to your Success Factor Snapshot
- Adaptability

Each of these five predictors of long-term success leads logically to a Key Question that can help you get straight to the heart of the candidate's ability to do your job.

Key Question #1

Would you please give me an example of a situation in which you have demonstrated initiative?

Top performers are self-motivated. They don't wait for the world to come to them; they strike out of their own accord in search of more. This is a lifelong pattern; it is not an anomaly.

Top 5% Talent are serial overachievers. The five-year-old who had the most successful lemonade stand on the block grows up to be the junior-high student who organizes a community anti-graffiti mural project at the school. A few years later, during the summer between high school graduation and the first year of college, the same young person recruits friends and family to build a Habitat for Humanity home. By college graduation (Cum Laude, of course), the Top 5% specimen has amassed a long history of extracurricular achievement and academic excellence.

Internal drive is the constant, and the goals and activities by which it is expressed are the variables. Top performers are always doing more than they are required to do.

If you can gather more than a handful of quick examples of initiative using the First Key Question, chances are you're speaking with somebody who has the self-motivation it will take to achieve your critical success factors.

We contend initiative is the most significant predictor of future success.

Key Question #2

Would you please give me an example of when you executed a project or a strategy flawlessly?

Top Talent doesn't make excuses. They do what it takes to get the job done. Goals are reached, and they are reached on time, in budget, to the stated metrics and measurements. Deadlines don't slip, because once the mission is set, Top 5% Talent gets moving. They don't lag, over-analyze, procrastinate, or second-guess.

This question is designed to give you insight into the candidate's ability to hit targets. Candidates who consistently execute flawlessly are able to meet their objectives in spite of all the problems, bottlenecks, roadblocks, speed bumps, and dysfunctional people that get in their way. They are able to find detours, blaze other paths, and marshal resources creatively to meet their primary objectives.

Key Question # 3

Tell me about your most successful accomplishment leading a cross-functional team on a major project or initiative.

No general ever won a battle alone. No captain of industry built an empire by himself in his back yard. Top 5% Talent understands how important it is to be able to build, lead, and motivate effective, cohesive teams. Team leadership is something at which they excel.

We are all good leaders in good times. The best leaders, however, are able to rally the troops and motivate people even when circumstances are difficult. From long-term steering committees to ad hoc "Tiger Teams," the ability to build consensus and direct the actions of several people at once is critical to success in nearly every high-level position.

A top candidate should be able to come up with a minimum of several examples of when they've built and led successful teams. The reason to ask about cross-functional teams is that most candidates immediately think about their formal department/group team. But strong leadership requires the ability to influence and motivate people *who are not directly under you* to engage with you to achieve a task, objective, mission, project, or outcome.

The last two Key Questions circle back to the Success Factor Snapshot for specifics, and they are both used to assess whether the candidate can achieve your Success Factors.

Key Question #4

> *One of our most critical objectives is <Success Factor/Outcome>. Would you please describe your most comparable accomplishment?*

Top performance is not a one-time event.

Comparable accomplishments and similar past successes demonstrate the ability do the job you need done. Before you extend a high-level job offer, you need to feel confident that the candidate can achieve the Success Factors you've outlined for the key role. "Comparable" is the operative term in this question. Comparable means similar in terms of scope, size, complexity, resources, budget, and timeframe.

Key Question #5

*Can you walk me through how you would you go about achieving
<Success Factor> in our environment?*

In all likelihood, the fifth key question will not arise until a second, third, or fourth interview. Don't expect a perfect answer; the candidate may not have all the information they need to answer it on the spot. This question, instead, is a springboard to dialogue.

This question hits upon a key success predictor that is frequently missed by CEOs and executives interviewing for key roles: Will this person be able to adapt to your specific situation, environment, or timeline? Does he understand what's different in terms of size, scope, teams, people, changes, standards, resources, values, culture, and so on? Does she ask intelligent questions and problem-solve to answer this question?

Sometimes the questions the candidate asks back are more important than any statement or example they might give. You should be evaluating the questions the candidate asks and the assumptions behind them. Are they approaching the question as if they will have the same support staff and budget as in their previous position—but your company is half (or twice) that size?

The only really wrong answer to this question is, "The same way I did it before." Unless circumstances, people, budgets, timelines, products, infrastructure and such are all the same...the candidate could not achieve success without making changes, assumptions, developing theory, speculation, conclusions and applying what they've learned in the past to a new situation.

Under The Magnifying Glass

After the first five key questions comes the more difficult task: validating the truth. We teach our clients to follow up with probing questions that make up what we call the Magnifying Glass Approach to interviewing.

In our corporate in-house workshops and speaking engagements with professional groups, we routinely ask executives, "What percentage of job applicants you've interviewed over the last few years do you believe either embellished or exaggerated what they had done or what they thought they were capable of doing?" Usually we hear a number between 100 to 125% (because many candidates embellish more than once).

While not every candidate is guilty of puffery, we know from experience that it happens. Candidates claim responsibility for accomplishments that really were not their accomplishments, but rather those of bosses, peers, or perhaps even subordinates.

There is a bulletproof solution to the problem of "accomplishment inflammation," and that is to become a great detective. When you learn to probe every answer for relevant details, you'll discover what we have: There hasn't been a candidate born who can make up false answers quickly enough. They've either done what they say they've done and can describe it in infinite detail, or they will implode in the chair right in front of you (and it's messy when it happens).

Every time you ask a candidate a question based on examples, expect to spend fifteen to thirty minutes exploring the details of each example. Put the candidate's answer under a magnifying glass, and ask for multiple examples to make sure something wasn't an anomaly.

Every interview will be different, but no matter what example is being discussed, your probes will generally follow the time-honored journalist's "5 *W*s":

- Who?
- What?
- When?
- Where?
- Why?
- For good measure, throw in How? (Yes, even though it is not a *W.*)

Train yourself to have a knee-jerk reaction to high-level, nonspecific answers. Usually, it's not that the candidate is trying to deceive you; it's that he or she simply hasn't thought to give concrete, detailed answers. You can help the candidate along by following up assertions and blanket statements with one of the following Magnifying Glass questions:

- "Could you give me an example of that?"
- "Can you be more specific about that?"
- "Can you give me a bit more information about that?"
- "What were the most important details about that situation?"
- "What was your responsibility within the project team?"
- "What did you personally do to ensure that success?"
- "Who else was involved in that project?"
- "Why did you take that approach on the project?"
- "Why did you pick those individuals to be on the team?"

Get all the details. Dates, numbers, names of people, schedules. Both of you will be helping each other to get to the facts faster and with more relevance.

Other good Magnifying Glass questions:

- What was your role in the project?
- What success was achieved?
- How did you decide what to do?
- Can you give me a few examples of your personal initiative on the project?
- When have you faced a comparable challenge?
- Where did the resources come from to get that accomplished?
- How were parameters for the project set?
- Would you consider that process a success? Why or why not? (Remember, even a failure has value.)
- When have you failed to meet your boss's expectations?
- How did the team make mid-course corrections?
- What did you learn specifically?
- With benefit of hindsight, what would you do differently next time?

Keep going until you know what you need to know. (Or until it becomes apparent the candidate is being elusive or downright lying. If this happens, it's time to cut and run.) Whatever you do, don't give in and assume it'll work out. Some candidates are great about changing the subject and making you think you got enough information. Be sure to make a note of what happened and then move on. (Our Web site contains a series of templates available for downloading, including a Magnifying Glass checklist.)

Homework Assignments: The Final Confirmation

When the pool of talent is narrowed down to the final two candidates, it's time for the interview team to come up with homework assignments. An important predictor of how a candidate will adapt to your organization's environment is to see an example of his or her thought processes, analytical skills, and problem-solving, up close and personal.

Effective homework assignments are projects of reasonable size and scope that involve one of the most critical Success Factors listed in your Success Factor Snapshot. The candidate should be given all the support he or she needs to adequately answer the question or complete the assignment. The candidate should then return to the interview panel and present results and conclusions, and lead a question and answer discussion based on the homework. No matter what functional area, homework should entail questioning, analysis, research, and a panel discussion with some form of presentation.

While homework assignments are "out there" in the hiring world, some candidates may object to doing what they perceive as unpaid work.

Most Top 5% Talent, because of their self-motivated nature, will be intrigued and embrace the challenge. But if they've had previous encounters with unscrupulous employers who actually *do* assign homework and go on to use candidate ideas (even though they did not hire the candidate) you'll need to reassure them that you aren't asking them to come up with the "right answer." Instead, you are looking for a concrete example of their approach to problems, their analytical and presentation skills, and their ability to synthesize information.

The scope of homework should be appropriate; that is, you shouldn't ask candidates to dedicate forty hours on nights and weekends to solving your most pressing problem as "homework." Make it clear at the outset that the homework is not going to be as deep as the actual job, and that you aren't looking so much for their answer as for deep insight into their thought and action processes.

Examples of Homework Possibilities

- "Bring in a (sales plan/board presentation/financial statement/ _____) you've created in a previous position; present it to the panel and be prepared to discuss it in detail. Of course, we are not asking you to breach confidentiality, so feel free to alter or disguise the data if you so choose."

- "Based on what you know of us and our needs, create a high-level strategy to address Success Factor X. We will, of course, give you access to the personnel and materials you need to be able to complete this assignment."

- "Take home this set of financial statements and analyze them. When you return, tell us where you see problems, and how you would go about fixing them."

- "Prepare a PowerPoint presentation on how you would begin to approach each Success Factor if you were offered the position."

- "Outline the steps you would take to create a vendor qualification program."

Homework is one of the best ways to assess how a candidate thinks and provides you with ancillary information about his current work environment, resources, communication capabilities, and insights into his strategy and planning techniques. Furthermore, homework demonstrates the candidate's ability to understand and adapt to the needs, wants, resources, and working environment of your company.

Some people are technically superior but poor interviewers; other people are fantastic in the interview but not so much when it comes to locking themselves in a room and tackling a problem. Homework levels the playing field and allows every final candidate the chance to demonstrate their aptitude and their work style in your environment.

Visit our Web site at to download additional samples of Homework Assignments: www.impacthiringsolutions.com.

A Homework Story

When you evaluate homework, it's important that you think not only in terms of the candidates' answers, but also how they arrived at them, and the assumptions that they made to begin.

A client company we worked with several years ago was searching for a new VP of Sales. The search had come down to two candidates: One from a much smaller organization, and one from a Fortune 500 firm.

The CEO of our client company had built the company in his own image, and it was a fast-moving, entrepreneurial, wild-wild-west environment. This was apparent everywhere—in the company literature, décor, dress code, and in the interview process as well.

The final two candidates were asked to answer one question as their homework: "How would you find new customers for our products?"

The Fortune 500 candidate returned with a detailed, precise PowerPoint presentation illustrating his strategy. There were charts related to industry trends, complicated graphics illustrating possible sales-building strategies, analysis, academic citations—the whole nine yards. The presentation was built just as though it would be presented to the executive team at a Fortune 500 company.

The CEO was not impressed. Although the reasoning and analysis was deep and wide, the presentation struck him as a "plan to make a plan." It was too high-level, too abstract. The CEO was concerned that the candidate, used to having an enormous cast of support personnel and resources, wouldn't be able to make the transition into doing many things himself.

The second candidate arrived with nothing but a stack of tattered industry and consumer magazines under his arm. There were paperclips scattered throughout the pages. He sat down with the CEO, flipped to the first paperclip, and said, "I'd definitely call on these guys. They manufacture products using similar materials; it's possible we could make a convincing argument that they should outsource some basic fabrication to us." He flipped to the next paperclip, and the next, and the next, explaining why he would pick up the phone and speak with each.

The CEO was impressed. The second candidate understood the need to roll up his sleeves, get dirty, and push. He didn't waste time creating an electronic presentation to explain what he wanted to do; he invested his time finding specific companies who might become customers.

The Fortune 500 candidate was able to strategize at a high level, but his homework demonstrated that he would not mesh well with the "Jump in and just do it" culture at our client. The job went to the second candidate.

It's not that the Fortune 500 candidate wasn't capable, that he didn't have past success or experience, or the right education, or wasn't a nice guy. The hiring team liked both of these candidates, but the homework project helped them assess and evaluate which of two qualified candidates would be more adaptable to their wants, needs, culture, and environment. They were able to make a hiring decision that was Success-Factor-based because they utilized a methodology that provided a more in-depth approach to interviewing.

The moral of the story is, don't be bowled over by the person whose presentation is the slickest. Look for evidence of ability to achieve within your environment and culture, and for evidence that the candidate's underlying approach to problem solving is sound.

Chapter Summary

❖ **The interviewing process must be structured** and use the Success Factor Snapshot to be as effective as possible.

❖ **Typical "fuzzy" interview questions, or travelogues of a candidate's resume, are useless** when it comes to predicting their ability to succeed in the job.

❖ **A relaxed candidate can interview better**; give them the benefit of the doubt and make them comfortable before digging in.

❖ The **Five Key Questions** should be the foundation of all interviews:

➤ Can you give me an example of initiative?

➤ When have you executed a project or strategy flawlessly?

➤ When have you successfully built and led a team?

➤ One of our critical Success Factors is X. Can you give me an example of a comparable achievement from your past?

➤ How would you go about achieving our Success Factor within this environment?

❖ The **Magnifying Glass Approach** to probing questions helps you to figure out who's really done the job vs. who's exaggerating.

❖ **Homework is a critical predictor** not only of ability to succeed, but also how a candidate will work within your environment.

Chapter 11: Beyond The Interview: Vetting, Verification, And Evaluating The Truth

> Trust, but verify.
>
> *Ronald Reagan*

Stay Focused When The Finish Line Is In Sight

The interview is over. The candidate has left the building. Now comes the hard part; making sense of what you've just heard. Assessment, verification, evaluation, and in-depth analysis of the candidate's stories and claims are on the docket for the interview team.

Do you have a systematic process to ensure the candidates have been truthful? How do you ensure you are continuing with the right candidate as you move through various interviews?

If you're like most hiring executives, when you interview a candidate, you scribbled a few notes in the resume margin. You formed a general impression based on a mélange of nonverbal cues and behaviors. You've already decided that you "like" or "don't like" the candidate. But you don't have a tool to help you compare apples to apples, and candidates to your Success Factor Snapshot.

The Water Cooler Is No Place To Debrief

We have frequently seen interviewers emerge from a round of interviews and then commiserate near the proverbial water cooler.

"So, what did you think of Candidate A?"

"Well, he seemed enthusiastic."

"She had a lot of energy."

"He was polite."

"Seemed okay. I think he could probably do the job."

If you have stuck with us this far, you will immediately recognize the problem with this kind of informal "debrief." These abstract impressions are not grounded in what's needed to succeed on the job.

A case in point from our experience: One of the best people a client of ours ever hired nearly wasn't invited back for a second interview. She was a powerhouse—highly accomplished, with more than enough demonstrable success behind her. In terms of her ability to do the job, she stood head and shoulders above all other candidates.

There was, however, a "problem." The candidate was not a fashion plate. The company's employees tended to be fashionable, with name-brand labels oozing out of every office suite. The candidate arrived at the first interview in a tasteful but conservative suit, her hair pulled back in a plain style, wearing minimal makeup. Some members of the interview panel (we never asked who, exactly) apparently fixated on her "lack of grooming."

When we spoke to the hiring team after the first interview and they expressed reluctance to continue interviewing the candidate, we were puzzled. It took considerable probing to uncover the fact that the interviewers who had expressed reservations were subconsciously prejudiced based on the candidate's "stodgy, plain" clothing and makeup.

We were flabbergasted. The position was not one that required interfacing with clients who would expect flash and style. She would be managing sophisticated financial analysis, planning, budgeting, and forecasting.

Here was a candidate with phenomenal qualifications who had nailed the answer to every question they gave her…but she wasn't "glam" enough?

We let the hiring committee know what a mistake they were making. The important question, we reminded them, was not whether this candidate subscribed to *Vogue* and *Elle*, shopped at Saks, or invested a fifth of her income in facials, French manicures, MAC makeup, or triple foil highlights. The important question—the only question—was whether she could do what the company needed done.

The hiring team rethought their position. The candidate was invited back, eventually offered the job, promoted twice, and last we knew, was still successfully making things happen nearly a decade later, Armani suit or no.

This episode crystallizes a universal truth about candidate evaluation: *Superficial, irrelevant issues often get more of an interviewer's attention than real substance.*

"Criteria" To Toss Out

When you interview, what's on your mental checklist? Some of the most time-honored "criteria" have absolutely nothing to do with whether a candidate can do the job.

- Strong presentation
- Assertive or Aggressive
- Manicured
- Polished shoes in the right color (brown with navy, not black)
- "Enthusiasm"
- High Energy
- Good eye contact
- Strong handshake
- Well-spoken
- Instant, unhesitant recall of events from many years ago (honestly, if somebody asked you about something that happened in 1993, wouldn't you pause and look up to the right as you tried to remember all the details?)
- Smooth speech without "ums" or stutters or backtracking
- Personable

Many hiring mistakes occur because the hiring team draws first impressions from factors like this, or because the candidate either wowed them or bored them during interviews. The team can lose sight of the real goal: Measuring the candidate's ability to deliver the results defined in the SFS.

You're not hiring an actor. You're hiring an Operations Director, or a VP of Finance, or a Plant Manager. In what way, exactly, does a candidate's handshake correlate with their ability to succeed in those jobs?

In some jobs, of course, presentation skills and a solid professional appearance are important. But focusing on "hot-button" factors like those in the list above does not help to select the right candidate.

The Eight-Dimension Success Matrix™

To eliminate interviewers' ingrained tendency to focus on superficial criteria and miss substantive evidence, we developed a structured tool to help each interviewer evaluate each candidate—objectively, fairly, and comprehensively.

The Eight-Dimension Success Matrix is the tool we have our clients use to rate "fit" based on the examples, illustrations, specifics, results, accomplishments, and patterns of behavior that emerge in candidate interviews.

It is quick to use, easy to understand, and focused on the job itself. Perhaps most importantly, it calibrates interviewer ratings, keeping everyone on the same page. Built around the five key predictors of success, the Eight-Dimension Success Matrix forces interviewers to assess answers to questions in a uniform way.

Accountability to the group is vital. When interviewers know they will have to justify the ratings assigned to each candidate to the entire group of interviewers—especially if they've designated Candidate A's Team Leadership ability 1 while everybody else assigned her a 2—the whole process is taken more seriously.

Because each member of the interviewing team fills out an Eight-Dimension Success Matrix form after each interview, by end of a long interview cycle a candidate's file may contain twenty or more forms. The full file allows the person with final hiring power to evaluate the full-spectrum of evaluation on all Success Factors. Skimming the right column helps the hiring executive to rapidly compare the same candidate interview-to-interview, and also to evaluate candidates' qualifications against each other, on equal footing.

How To Use The Form

The most important consideration in using the matrix is this: **Do Not, Under Any Circumstances, Put Off Completing The Form After Each Interview.** Human memory fades rapidly four to six hours after an event. Once details are gone from short-term memory, they are lost forever.

You absolutely must ensure that your hiring process does not fall victim to procrastination and memory loss ("Er, gee, I think this was the guy with the orange tie who used to work at Enron, yeah? Or was that Exxon? Shoot, I don't remember…")

The hiring team leader must make sure each interviewer sits down immediately after the interview (or by that same day's end, at the latest) to complete the sections for which they have gathered enough information.

It is almost certain that no interviewer will be able to fill out an entire matrix after just one interview. That's fine. Notes about sections that require more information and what questions to ask in subsequent interviews can be written in the "Comments" area, or on the back of the form.

Eight-Dimension Success Matrix™

Date	Candidate	Position

Dimensions	0 **Less Than Required**	1 **Meets Requirements**
Work History and Eduction	Relevant, success-based experience and education fall short in critical areas.	Background and years of experience consistent with needs of position. Work history and education are adequate.
High Initiative and Self-Motivation	Lacks initiative and self-motivation. Not Proactive. Waits to be told what to do.	Adequate. Some good examples of taking initiative and being proactive. Examples are aligned in areas of the SFS.
Flawless Execution	Misses goals and objectives. Budgets are not hit. Deadlines are frequently extended.	Can achieve execution necessary for minimum success in the position. Solid examples of executing difficult projects.
Leadership of Teams	Poor to inadequate levels of team leadership. No comprehension how to leverage team.	Size and scope of teams managed meet the needs of the position. Solid ability to leverage results through different types of teams.
Similar Success (SFS)	Few of the critical Success Factors will be met.	Has met similar expectations in the past, or understands precisely what needs to be done.
Adaptability	Does not understand differences in resources, constraints; no evidence of adaptability.	Asked good questions, understands critical differences, evidence of adaptability in past.
Personality and Style	Unbridgeable mismatch between candidate and culture or manager. Highly unlikely to ever be able to work constructively given mismatch.	Appropriate fit; personality and style in alignment. No major behavioral problems or issues observed.
Cultural and Team Fit	Unbridgeable gap between past company culture / work style and hiring company's team culture. Gap is too large to risk.	Past cultures and environments similar. Should work well with others in the organization.

Eight-Dimension Success Matrix™

Interviewer	Comments	
2 **Exceeds** **Requirements**	**3** **Greatly** **Exceeds Requirements**	**Score**
Background and years are consistent with position. Additional experience and/or education might be valuable.	Background and years exceed the requirements of position. Good for fast-track or additional responsibility. Broad experience in a variety of companies/roles.	0 1 2 3 ○ ○ ○ ○
Frequently will go beyond the call of duty. High initiative and very strong self-motivation. Proactively exceeds requirements of the job.	Initiative and self-motivation are apparent in all positions. Consistently takes the lead and will go until results are met. May have to hold back.	0 1 2 3 ○ ○ ○ ○
Always hits and occasionally exceeds execution expectations. Well regarded for ability to consistently deliver flawlessly. Recognized for contributions.	Frequently exceeds expectations for execution. Usually considered the "go-to" person when something must absolutely be executed flawlessly. Wins Awards.	0 1 2 3 ○ ○ ○ ○
Great team leadership. Always accomplishes results with teams. Track record of leading cross-functional teams.	Exceeds requirements. Frequently gets the tough team projects. Strong recognition for exceptional team leadership. Outstanding motivator.	0 1 2 3 ○ ○ ○ ○
Track record of hitting and sometimes exceeding similar Success Factors.	Consistently exceeds expectations. Exceeds almost all of the Success Factors.	0 1 2 3 ○ ○ ○ ○
Excellent, demonstrated ability to adapt to new situations. Clearly understands key differences from prior environments and culture.	Can easily adapt and will likely change the environment. Proven "change agent" recognized for ability to change culture around them.	0 1 2 3 ○ ○ ○ ○
Fits in well with everyone. Well-liked. Could easily work with managers, subordinates. Strong communicator.	Extraordinary communicator and relationship-builder. Very comfortable and likeable. Borders on charismatic, inspirational.	0 1 2 3 ○ ○ ○ ○
Well liked by hiring team. Good fit on values and cultural match. Highly comparable prior cultures and teams.	Fits culture and environment like a glove. Extremely strong prior similar culture and teams. Will fit in from day one.	0 1 2 3 ○ ○ ○ ○

We highly recommend that somebody on the interviewing team—preferably the hiring manager—be charged with distributing *and collecting* the Eight-Dimension Success Matrix forms before and after each round of interviews. When people know they'll be held accountable at the end of the day, they won't put off what needs to be done.

While there are few rules about using the Matrix, there are several tips to keep in mind.

- The form should be explained and discussed fully among the team *before* interviews begin.
- Each interviewer should understand the difference between a score of Zero, 1, 2, and 3.
- Each interviewer should understand what each of the Factors is intended to measure.
- **A candidate who rates Zeros** in any category is probably not the best choice for the job.
- The "sweet spot" on the Eight-Dimension Success Matrix form is a ranking of "2." Not too hot or too cold—just right.
- Depending on the job, it is possible that **a candidate with one or two ratings of "1"** might still be up to the job.
- **A candidate whose Matrix scores are consistently "3" across the board is likely overqualified.** At a minimum you might encounter a fair level of difficulty retaining this individual. He or she would probably become bored with the job and is therefore NOT always a good choice.
- **Your hiring team should discuss their rankings** of the final candidates in great detail to make sure no questions or concerns are left unaddressed.

You may download this form in PDF format from our Web site, www.impacthiringsolutions.com.

When References Go Bad

If a candidate makes it to the second round of interviews, it's getting serious. You've settled on one or possibly two candidates. You believe with all your heart, soul, and mind that one is the right person for the job. He or she seems to be the cherry on the sundae, and you're looking forward to making the job offer to the number one candidate.

You phone HR and tell them to make two quick reference calls based on names and numbers the candidate has given you. Once that's done, you figure, it's a wrap.

Stop right there.

Even though most reference calls tend to be five-minute, rubber stamp, "Is-he-a-nice-guy/would-you-rehire-her/did-she-do-well" conversations, *yours* will not be. Your calls won't even technically be "reference calls." They will be twenty to thirty minutes long. They will go into great detail. They will be deep third-party verifications of what the candidate has told you in the interviews. You will push and probe for nearly as much detail with each reference as you did with the candidate.

You must do so, not because you do not trust this person (it's obvious that you do, or you wouldn't be on the cusp of offering him a job), but because verification is a mandatory step in a proven hiring process.

Ordinary reference calls (and even background checks—more on that in a moment) don't get to the heart of potential problems. Most people who receive reference calls expect to be on the line for fewer than ten minutes. They expect to be able to say simple things like, "Cathy is a great worker! You can't go wrong hiring her. I'd rehire her in an instant."

But you, as the hiring company, are about to invest literally hundreds of thousands of dollars in a new hire. To do so without fully verifying what the candidate has told you would be irresponsible.

Up until now, you've had only the candidate's word to go on. References, though, are a treasure chest waiting to be opened and explored.

Finding The Right Reference

First off: No family, friends, or personal references. While many applicants still include these in their list, personally invested people are unlikely to yield much useful information. When a reference's primary relationship with a candidate is personal, there is an automatic conflict of interest. Their loyalty is to the candidate, not you, and most importantly, they are unlikely to be able to speak intelligently about the candidate's work accomplishments.

Once you've decided you want to hire a particular candidate, ask them for three to five professional references. Ideally, these should be former bosses, peers, or individuals they have supervised. We suggest to our search clients that reference checks should be conducted on a 360-degree basis, including all the individuals who might touch this person, both inside and outside the company. Ask for the numbers of key customers, vendors, and suppliers.

If the candidate is still employed at a company where they have been for a long time (five years or more), and they would prefer you do not contact their boss until an offer is made, work around it as best you can. Perhaps a former mentor from another department has left the company and would be able to speak about them. Maybe the person who hired them originally and saw them through their meteoric first four years is now retired and living in Key West—call her.

A Top 5% candidate, if he or she is interested in the job, will work with you on this, and may even agree to let you contact a current employer under certain circumstances. As a last resort, sometimes candidates will grant you permission to talk with their boss once an offer is formally presented. You can always make the offer contingent upon the successful outcome of reference checks.

Because coworkers and colleagues have usually spent more time with the candidate than the boss, they are outstanding sources of verification. Usually "lateral" references can offer deeper insights into work style, team leadership ability, personality, and cultural issues. Pay particular attention to these areas when speaking to former coworkers, probing for any indications that the person may pose interpersonal problems or "rub people the wrong way."

Going Deeper: Secondary References

Don't stop at the first layer of verification. When you speak to first-tier references (those whose names the candidate gave you), ask *whom else* the candidate worked with, reported to, supervised, or led as part of a team. These are secondary references, and they are additional potential sources of objective verification.

Then, go back to the candidate and ask them whether they would mind if you contacted these secondary references. A highly qualified candidate will usually agree immediately.

If you sense hesitation, it may be a red flag. If the candidate objects to contacting a secondary reference, ask why. Sometimes they will offer a good reason (*"I was charged with supervising the team's efforts. His department was always late with their deliverables and I had to ride him hard for a year to make sure he followed up on his commitments. I don't think Judy, my primary reference, was aware of the ongoing friction between our departments, but Bob in accounting was on the same team. Would you like me to put you in touch with him?"*). Other times, they will be vague and evasive (*"Um, well, we didn't work together much and she didn't have anything to do with my projects. I don't think she'd really be able to tell you much."*) Listen carefully to the answers you receive from the candidate and make an informed judgment call before proceeding with a secondary reference verification interview.

As a rule of thumb, if you get strong verification not only from a candidate's "first tier" of references, but also from secondary references, you can almost bet the farm you've found the candidate you're looking for. (Almost. See "Background Checks" before you leap, though.)

Finally, it is important not to "wear out" references. Third-party verification calls should be one of the last items on the hiring agenda, not the first. Not even the middle. Our Eight-Point Success Validation form is lengthy and intense and will take at least thirty minutes to complete; this is a significant investment of time, and you should let people know up front that the call will take this long.

A good third of the information you need about candidates is obtained in verification phone calls. It's best to set expectations early in a reference phone call. Make it clear that you are *not* asking for a recommendation. Rather, you are verifying information that you've been given, and you would appreciate as much detail as the reference feels comfortable giving.

The template that follows can help you to guide a third-party verification call. It is not a script, but a suggested structure to help you decide what to ask and what to probe further.

You may download this form in PDF format from our Web site, www.impacthiringsolutions.com.

Eight-Point Validation Form™

Reference Name _____   Company   _____

Reference Title _____   Contact Info _____

Critical Issues	Relative Questions	Answer Helps To...	Comments
Work History and Education	What were the candidate's background, positions, and reporting relationships? Was the candidate promoted? Did the candidate receive any additional training? Are there other highlights from candidate's employment?	Verify the candidate's background and years of past experience as they relate to the open position. Verify levels of responsibility and future "promote-ability."	
High Initiative and Self-Motivation	Can you provide some examples of how the candidate took initiative to produce results? Did the candidate proactively meet or exceed the needs of the job?	Verify the candidate's initiative and whether self-motivation is strong enough to meet your needs. Verify how often the candidate went beyond the call of duty.	
Flawless Execution	Could you describe, in detail, how the candidate was able to achieve success and meet expectations for a position? Can you provide some solid examples of the candidate's execution on difficult projects? Was the candidate recognized for his/her contributions? Did he or she receive any awards?	Verify whether the candidate consistently met and/or occasionally exceeded execution expectations. Verify the candidate's ability to learn, adjust, and compensate to consistently deliver flawlessly. Verify level and frequency of exceeding expectations.	
Leadership of Teams	Would you please describe the size and scope of teams the candidate managed and how these related to the organizational chart? Can you give me one or two concrete examples of when the candidate led teams to achieve difficult tasks?	Verify the candidate's team leadership abilities. Verify the candidate's track record of leading cross-functional teams. Verify the candidate's ability to build and motivate others within the organization.	

Eight-Point Validation Form™			
Critical Issues	**Relative Questions**	**Answer Helps To...**	**Comments**
Similar Success (SFS)	Can you share one or two significant achievements this candidate had during tenure? (Probe for specific details: dates, people involved, issue at hand, steps taken, and results). Identify two or three of the most critical Success Factors that you want met. "We need _____ accomplished. Do you think he/she is up to the task? Why or why not?" Can you provide me with specific examples of the candidate's performance vs. expectations?	Verify the candidate's representation of same events in the interview. Verify track record of meeting and sometimes exceeding similar expectations. Verify examples and details to be sure the candidate's responses are in line with references responses. Verify past expectations with the candidate's documentation of his/her performance.	
Adaptability	How well did the candidate adapt to his/her new position when first hired? What were the major obstacles? What resources/budgets were available to the candidate? Was the candidate instrumental in helping others adapt?	Verify excellent ability to adapt to new situations. Clarifies key differences from prior environments and cultures. Verify ability to adapt and adjust to key differences in available resources. Verify whether the candidate was able to assist others with adaptations/changes.	
Personality and Style	Whom did the candidate interact with on a regular basis? Was the candidate well liked by the team/others? How well did the candidate communicate with others? Did the candidate develop strong relationships with others?	Verify scope of influence within organization, including levels of management. Verify how well the candidate got along with others in the organization. Verify communication style and rapport to your organization.	
Cultural and Team Fit	Could you please describe the company culture and environment during candidate's tenure? For example, was it fast paced, entrepreneurial, corporate, laid-back, friendly?	Compare previous culture with your company culture and environment. Assess appropriateness of "fit" with your firm.	

Testing And Assessment

In 2004, a Pennsylvania-based consulting firm (Development Dimensions International) ascertained that 83% of hiring managers use testing as a part of the hiring process. This number is nearly double what it was in 1999. Assessment has become a part of the corporate hiring landscape, for better or worse.

We believe testing is a valuable adjunct to the Success Factor Methodology, because when administered correctly, tests can uncover useful information about personality traits, potential for high achievement, and other factors that may not be immediately evident in an interview situation. However, there are several cautions about assessment instruments.

We highly recommend that our clients use an outside, third-party assessment professional who is specifically trained to select appropriate tests, as well as administer and interpret the results. Beyond using appropriate personnel, we advise the following:

1. **The instrument must be appropriate to the job.** Each selected test should measure traits, characteristics, and skills that are directly and obviously relevant to the job. If you are hiring a Finance VP, for example, there is an obvious reason to measure his or her basic intelligence with a standard IQ test. Other appropriate scales may be honesty, integrity, and ethics—important qualities for the person who will be in charge of the company coffers. On the other hand, there is no apparent reason to administer an instrument like the Minnesota Multiphasic Personality Inventory, which is designed to test for mental and emotional disorders.

2. **The instrument must be valid and reliable.** The Buros Institute, an organization founded in 1935 to catalog and evaluate psychological tests, publishes two comprehensive directories that can help you to select instruments that are known to be reliable and valid. *The Mental Measurements Yearbook* and *Tests In Print* are available at most libraries

and contain descriptions and reviews of psychological instruments. Be sure to ask consulting industrial psychologists whether the assessments they use are listed in these directories. If you are interested in how they were developed and validated, you can consult these reference works. At last count, the volumes had collected development, price, administration, and interpretation data on more than 11,000 instruments.

3. **Be wary of free online tests.** Unless they come from a highly regarded institute and/or are listed in one of the books mentioned above, they may not be valid and reliable instruments.

4. **The instrument must be administered and interpreted professionally.** We cannot emphasize enough that tests, inventories, personality profiles, and the like are difficult to interpret for a nonprofessional. Human Resources professionals are generally not qualified to administer psychological or behavioral tests. If you do choose to use some form of assessment to help you make a hiring decision, it is safer and more effective to delegate responsibility (and potential liability) to a third party, who will likely ask candidates to sign waivers before taking the tests. These professionals will also ensure that untrained people on the hiring team do not focus on one or two potentially "negative" findings in a twenty-page report—something we have seen frequently.

Some companies choose to administer personality tests only after the job is offered and accepted. The purpose in this case is not to select the "best" candidate, but rather to aid in the new hire's transition to a new position. If the inventories identify potential personality or communication style mismatches among the new employee and her superiors and/or subordinates, all parties can be briefed on each other's styles ahead of time, and needless conflicts can be avoided.

Background Checks

Finally, we reach the granddaddy of all pre-hiring due diligence: The Background Check. As with psychological and personality testing, we believe this is an activity best left to trained professionals who understand the legal and ethical constraints of such activities.

Background checks are often the last shield between a hiring company and a particularly slick candidate who interviews well. You might be surprised at how many people misrepresent their educational credentials, for example. In recent years, the media has exposed numerous scandals resulting from puffery in nearly every sector.

- In 2004, Quincy Troupe, poet laureate of the State of California and a tenured college professor, resigned his post. The reason? He had lied for years about his background, listing himself as a graduate of Grambling University. In fact, the professor (who was in charge of training graduate students, among other duties) had never even finished a bachelor's degree.
- Jeffrey Papows, former president of Lotus Software, was revealed by a 1999 *Wall Street Journal* investigation to have habitually exaggerated his past and accomplishments. While he claimed to be an orphan who rose through military ranks to eventually earn a Ph.D. from Pepperdine, he in fact had parents living in Massachusetts and a Ph.D. from a correspondence school. (He did, however, have a Master's from Pepperdine.)
- Sandra Baldwin, former president of the United States Olympic Committee, resigned after admitting that she had lied on her resume about earning a Ph.D from Arizona State University. She had not.
- Joseph Ellis, a Pulitzer Prize–winning biographer and professor of history at Mt. Holyoke College, was immensely popular for courses that included his personal insights into the violence and mayhem he had witnessed in Vietnam. In 2001, however, the *Boston Globe* exposed him: Dr. Ellis had

never left the States during the Vietnam War.

- In 2002, Veritas Software lost its Chief Financial Officer, Kenneth Lonchar, who resigned after his employer found out he had lied about his education, including an MBA from Stanford. He never earned such a degree. The company's stock plummeted in the weeks following these revelations.

There are many more cases like these. We could fill ten pages with just *recent* examples of resume-padding gone horribly wrong.

Obviously all these people were highly accomplished, but their basic dishonesty about degrees and other background information introduced high levels of doubt about their overall ethics and trustworthiness.

If such visible and respected organizations can be successfully bluffed in their highest-level hires, it can happen to your organization, too. The only way to be sure everything you've heard is true is to invest the time and money to verify the candidate's claims on his resume or other documents he completes and signs after beginning the interviewing process.

A Comprehensive Background Check

Many third-party providers can run a comprehensive background check to make sure there are no skeletons in any closet. These companies are fully up-to-date on laws that regulate the extent to which such checks can be used prior to employment.

If you decide to wait to run these checks until after you extend an offer, be sure you make the offer contingent upon satisfactory results from the background check.

- **Criminal Background.** In rare cases, charming and charismatic characters who just happen to be crooks have made their way all the way into positions of power. In our own experience, we know of a candidate who was offered a position as CFO without a criminal check. It was revealed later—too late—that he was under active investigation by the FBI and had allegedly embezzled huge sums of money in the past. A criminal background check would have revealed these issues before the company hired him, no mater how charming and convincing he had been in interviews.

- **Credit.** For any candidate who will be placed in a role where they will have access to the company coffers (or even something as innocent as a company credit card), we strongly recommend a credit check. Does the person have a huge amount of debt in the form of mortgages and consumer debt? Does the person make their required payments in a timely manner? Has the person filed for bankruptcy? What is their credit score? We realize that nobody is perfect, and while a high level of debt does not automatically disqualify a candidate, nor does the occasional late payment, there is merit in being cautious and checking these items. Financial pressure and stress can cause even the most well intentioned people to snap. Knowing a high-level executive's financial straits up front can help to head off potential problems.

- **Educational Background.** It may not actually be important to the job whether somebody earned an MBA or simply attended a year of a program without finishing. However, dishonesty about educational achievement is a huge red flag that should cause you to dig much deeper in every other area. If a candidate lies about this accomplishment, what else might he or she be lying about? Because educational background is frequently misrepresented, this check is the most likely place where you will uncover discrepancies. Integrity matters. We never recommend going forward with a candidate who has lied about their education.

- **State Drivers' License Bureau.** If a candidate has a record of arrests for driving under the influence, reckless accidents, or other egregious traffic violations, it may be a hint of deeper problems—and potential liability or risk to the company.

- **Social Security Verification.** Social Security will identify the names associated with the candidate's social security number. While most discrepancies can be cleared up quickly (marriage or adoption changed the last name, or a religious conversion changed the entire name), multiple aliases may be a red flag and should be explained by the candidate.

Chapter Summary

❖ **Don't trust—verify.** Throughout the interview process, you've taken the candidate's word on faith. Now it's time to move from faith to proof.

❖ **Evaluate candidates using the Eight-Point Success Matrix.** This standardized form helps the interviewing committee stay focused and objective and eliminates subconscious (irrelevant) biases. It also minimizes the ability of "good actors" to bluff their way into a role.

❖ **Make reference calls to verify candidate claims, not to request recommendations.** Good calls will take time and will dig nearly as deep as the interview itself.

❖ **If you test, use external psychologists who are professionally trained in testing and assessment.** Untrained personnel can expose you to liability and will not be able to guide you through the pitfalls and minefields of psychological tests.

❖ **Run thorough background checks.** As recent scandals have shown, you simply cannot take people's word for it. Verify everything. Better safe than deceived.

SECTION 4: CLOSING THE DEAL
Chapter 12: It's Never About The Compensation

> Do What You Love And The Money Will Follow.
>
> *Marsha Sinetar*

What Motivates Top Talent?

Over the last twenty years in our executive search practice, we've interviewed well over 10,000 candidates. We've discovered that top talent is motivated to leave their current job for one primary reason. That reason is *not* money.

By far, the most common motivation for Top 5% talent to consider leaving their current role is that they are not challenged, intellectually stimulated, or fulfilled in their current role. Some are bored out of their minds.

The first strategy of this talented group is usually to attempt to change their current job to get back on track for higher personal growth and impact. Failing that, not one will be willing to put their career on hold for an extended period of time. They will begin to seek greener pastures.

What's Maslow Got To Do With It?

In 1954, Abraham Maslow, considered the father of American humanistic psychology, proposed a revolutionary model of human motivation based on the known biographies of high-achievers— people he called "Self-Actualizers." (We call them Top 5% Talent.)

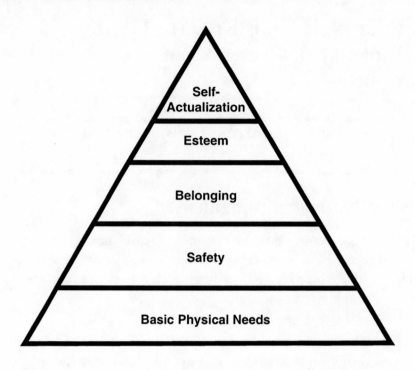

Among the people he studied were Jane Adams, Albert Einstein, Thomas Jefferson, Abraham Lincoln, Eleanor Roosevelt, and Albert Schweitzer. Based on his research, he proposed that all humans have several sets of needs, and that as we satisfy one level of needs, we are able to move "up" the hierarchy into a search for ways to meet higher-level needs.

The lowest level of Maslow's hierarchy (depicted as a pyramid to indicate the foundational nature of the lower needs) consists of basic physical needs—food, shelter, water, sanitation, and so on.

If we are hungry and cold and stuck outdoors in the freezing rain, the theory goes, we will dedicate all of our efforts and energy to meet the need for heat, food and shelter. We will *not* sit down and begin painting or writing a poem, or strike up an idle conversation with an attractive member of the opposite sex. Those higher-level activities must wait until the first level of needs is met.

Safety comes next; once we're dry, warm, and well fed, we tend to turn our attention to activities that will ensure such a state of affairs continue. We build a house, put locks on the doors, collect a store of firewood, dig a well so we'll never go thirsty again, and stock the pantry.

After these two levels of need are taken care of, humans start tending to their social or "belonging" needs—the need to be a part of groups that share common interests (think tanks, churches, civic organizations, sports teams, or fan organizations). Only *then* do they turn their attention to the kinds of needs that can be fulfilled by a career—the respect and esteem of others (family, friends, and coworkers).

Most people are lucky to make it to this point in the hierarchy. But Top Talent is a breed apart. Maslow himself speculated that only 2% of people would ever reach the point where they are able to strive for self-actualization, which is the highest human need.

Self-actualization is the key to understanding what motivates top talent: These people crave the opportunity to become more, accomplish more, achieve more, and earn profound self-worth from a difficult job done well. Their needs cannot be satisfied with a paycheck or a specific title. They want to make a difference, leave a legacy, and reach a level of knowing that demonstrates they are now "giving back."

If you can appeal to this deep-rooted need for self-actualization, in top talent, their gut will be saying, "I'd do this job for free."

Too often, we've seen hiring executives attempt to lure in a top performer by throwing money at them. While money may motivate people at the lower end of the need scale (administrative staff, entry-level employees, trainees, and middle managers without the ambition to rise further), the number one reason a Top 5% candidate will take your job is *not* the extra few thousand dollars a year you can offer him or her.

Money and benefits are second-level needs on Maslow's Hierarchy (Safety needs). If you want to convince a top performer to jump ship from where they are, you must be ready and able to convince them that at your organization, in your open position, they will be able to pursue their *highest personal aspirations for achievement.* They will find in your company the chance to become self-actualized.

They must believe that they will learn more, think harder, grapple with bigger challenges, and slay bigger dragons than they ever could hope to if they stayed where they are now.

They must be convinced that their accomplishments, one to three years down the road, will surpass those they could have made in their current position if they chose to stay put.

Understanding this concept is key to hiring Top Talent—especially Sleepers and Selective candidates. These people are already happy, because their basic physical, belonging, and esteem needs are already met. They've got the nice house, the great family, and the impressive title. They may not even realize (yet) that they're bored—or at some level unfulfilled.

If you hope to attract them to your firm, you must be able to use the interview to create visions of their best, highest-achieving self.

Three Reasons Top Talent Will Take Your Job

During our recruiting sessions, we experience a number of responses when speaking with potential candidates. When a Sleeper candidate discovers he is speaking with a recruiter, the first knee-jerk reaction is often hesitancy. After we introduce ourselves and explain the reason for our call, they usually say something like, "I'm happy where I am. I like my boss, and this job is fine." They'll usually add something along the lines of, "It would have to be *really* good to get me to make a change," or "Okay, let me close my door."

The magic words we use to get the conversation rolling are, "What if?"

- What if you could expand your circle of influence in a larger company?
- What if you could directly affect the growth and success of a young, dynamic tech startup?
- What if you had the chance to be responsible for taking a company public?
- What if you could have a significant impact on the bottom line?
- What if you could use all your creative talent with few, if any, restrictions?
- What if a new position gave you the potential to really put to use some of the talents you just don't have a chance to use right now?

In our experience, three aspects of a new position will motivate a candidate to make a move—and in rare cases, even take a pay cut.

Attraction #1: The Opportunity

Just as aggressive investors are willing to make safety tradeoffs for the chance to earn greater returns in the long run, Top 5% Talent candidates are more willing than most people to invest in their career by walking away from short-term comfort for potentially higher rewards.

We've known people who have taken a salary cut because they felt that the new position offered far more potential for achievement, experience, mentorship, learning, impact, and scope of influence. For these individuals, doing what they love is more important that a few thousand dollars. Doing what they love, making a difference, accomplishing something significant or helping others to become the best they can be means more than stagnating or managing the status quo.

In fact, we're willing to bet that most of the leaders reading this book know exactly what we mean and understand that true job satisfaction is priceless.

If you have done a good job constructing the Success Factor Snapshot, that single document becomes your primary selling tool in the early stages of recruiting. It shows candidates, in concrete terms, the "big picture." That document will help them to imagine themselves stepping into the role and making things happen.

One good technique to use in early recruiting calls is to ask questions based on the Success Factor Snapshot. Especially if a candidate is sitting on the fence, this is a good way to pique their interest.

> *"Candidate, you've told me you're relatively happy where you are. Let me ask you: If our open position offered you the chance to expand your career, meet your goals faster and allowed the opportunity to impact the company's bottom line, would you be willing to spend just five minutes to discuss it?"*

Nine out of ten times, the answer is "let me close my door." Nothing in this conversation had anything to do with money.

Next, using the Success Factor Snapshot you can probe to discover and entice with questions that will intrigue the candidate and will differentiate your firm from all others. Ask:

> *"In your current job, are you making personal, meaningful contributions in <Success Factor 1>? Are you challenged every day by the potential to <Success Factor 2>? Does your position use all of your talents and skills to <Success Factor 3>? Do you feel you are stretching and learning every day in order to <Success Factor 4?>"*

By the end of these questions, a Top 5% candidate will be thinking hard about where they are, where they're going, what they're getting out of their current position, and whether they can get more of the "good stuff" by making a change into your open position.

Attraction #2: The Company

In the beginning, the opportunity itself will be the best bait to attract a strong candidate to come in for a first interview. However, the emphasis soon shifts to the organization.

Most candidates will start with the company's Web site and check the reputation of the firm prior to coming in for an interview. Nobody climbs aboard a sinking ship. And nobody volunteers to take a trip unless they know the destination.

Your job, as the hiring executive, is to make it clear to the candidate that the ship—your company—is sound, exciting, and has all the amenities they could possibly require during their voyage with you.

During the interview process, you must create such a compelling vision for the future of the organization that the candidate can actually see, hear, touch, and taste success. Does the strategic plan call for innovation and growth into markets where the candidate has never had the chance to play? Highlight that and get her to start speculating about how she'll approach those unique challenges.

Will you expand into international markets in the next two years?

Is the R&D department working on a product that no other competitor will possibly be able to match?

Share your enthusiasm.

So, *why should somebody come to work for you?*

If you don't have an instantaneous, exciting, compelling answer, you need to revisit the Compelling Marketing Statement for the open position. You know your company is a great place to work: If it weren't, you wouldn't be there yourself. So communicate all the reasons you wake up every morning excited to come to the office.

Your enthusiasm will be contagious if you can offer candidates as much detail about the Company Vision as they offer you about their past success.

Attraction #3: The Boss

If it's the job opportunity itself that opens the door, and the company vision that gets them through the door, then it's generally the boss that makes or breaks the deal.

As an executive, the best influence you have over whether a candidate and their future boss "click" is to keep the hiring manager focused on the Company's Vision, the Success Factors, and the impact his new hire will make on the entire firm.

- **Top 5% Talent wants a leader who will both challenge and mentor them**—somebody who can work with them to make the absolute most of their talents and abilities.
- **Top candidates want a boss who is better than (not equal to) them.** If they feel they will not be able to learn from their new boss, they have little reason to leave their current job (where they probably could run the department themselves).
- **They want to be comfortable with the person they will interact with**, work with, and occasionally butt heads with day after day. If your highest level of management needs a bit of remedial work in communication skills, rapport, and empathy, there's no time like the present to put them through appropriate training to start refining those critical "people skills." Nobody wants to work for a drill sergeant or a tyrant, and if you are attempting to hire Top Talent to fill a position that's seen heavy turnover, you should make sure the problem is not the supervisor.

The Boss is the one true "wild card" in the motivational equation. Whether or not the direct supervisor and the best candidate will "click" is in many ways beyond your control as a CEO. The best that you can do is making sure the eventual boss understands how important they are to the success or failure of the search.

Finally, especially if that boss is *you*, keep in mind the Success Factors and the Compelling Marketing Statement. Make the candidate feel special. Use subtle language to get the candidate thinking in terms of *when*, not *if*, they join the team. There is a significant psychological shift that should begin immediately if you believe you've found your new hire. Use phrases like "you'll enjoy _____ here." Or "When you're on board, we'll appreciate your ability to _____."

Paving the way to a successful offer begins with the first phone call and ends when the candidate begins his first day. Paving the way to a successful working relationship begins with understanding that top performers need more than money and will remain for years if he can attain self-actualization. Make it so for each new hire.

Chapter Summary

❖ **High achievers don't just want more money.** While financial incentives may be a nice addition to an overall eventual offer, Top 5% Talent is a rare group, motivated to reach the top of Maslow's Hierarchy of needs: Self-Actualization.

❖ **"What if..."** is the magic phrase to use early in the process to get great candidates thinking about strong, compelling reasons why they should make a move.

❖ **The Success Factor Snapshot** shows candidates a big picture view of all they can become if they accept your offer. Use this to motivate them and build enthusiasm.

❖ **Candidates take new positions for three reasons: The Opportunity, The Company, and The Boss.** It's your job as the company leader to make sure each is enticing, interesting, and realistic.

Chapter 13: How To Make An Offer They'll Refuse

> In baseball, you must touch all the bases. Even if the batter knocks the ball out of the park, if he doesn't touch every base he won't score.
>
> *Zig Ziglar*

One of our most important rules for making any offer is this: You should never make an offer unless you are absolutely sure it will be accepted.

In this chapter, we will cover reliable techniques that let you turn the entire interview process into an extended dress rehearsal for an offer that is a foregone conclusion, based on your terms.

We have consulted in the past with many firms who, compared to their competition, had abysmal hiring success rates. There's absolutely no reason a candidate should *ever* say "No" to an offer; much like a marriage proposal, if you have any doubt whatsoever about the answer, it's either too soon or too late to ask.

In our experience, few hiring executives understand there are reliable steps they can take to ensure their top choice will ultimately accept an offer.

Here's an exceptional case from our files—it's a true story (we've omitted names to protect the guilty). Our client was a $120 million manufacturing firm located in Southern California. They brought us in because they were losing a full 60% of their first-choice candidates *after the offer*. Yes, you read that right: their hiring success ratio in hiring was a paltry 40%.

After discussing the unsuccessful hires with their CEO, we understood what was happening.

There was a major disconnect between the HR department, which handled hiring, and the interviewing managers. Nobody was actually managing the offer of employment process. Nobody was addressing concerns, smoothing over objections, or looking for potential sticking points. Nobody was making sure the candidates didn't accept a counteroffer and stay right where they were, only with a higher salary than before.

The HR Manager sincerely believed his job was to source candidates and then go directly to the offer paperwork. He was great at the preliminaries: running the ad, screening the incoming resumes, arranging interviews, and presenting candidates to the hiring manager. Then, he dropped out of the process entirely and waited to hear from the hiring manager about which candidate had "won."

At that point, the HR Manager helped to determine a salary and benefits package, drew up all the necessary paperwork, and put it in the mail to the candidate. Then and only then did he pick up the phone and call the candidate. The entire process was based on a presumptive close.

"Congratulations. We want to hire you. Your offer letter is in the mail. You'll receive $127,500 in annual salary, two weeks paid vacation, medical and life insurance after your first six months, a 401(k) plan with 3% company match after the first year, and an assigned parking spot in our garage. We would like you to start in two weeks. Possibly sooner. Any questions?"

He was baffled about why 6 out of 10 candidates that had made it through the interviewing process would turn the offer down. After all, wasn't that what the candidate was waiting for?

We were aghast. "Did you ever ask *why* they turned you down?"

The HR Manager's response was, "Um, no, not really. I just move on and extend the same offer to the number two candidate. If they're still available, they usually take it." The company was settling for its second choice most of the time simply because nobody knew how to talk their candidates through to a successful offer.

As we worked with the company to fix their problems, we discovered the HR Manager was understandably very insecure about the process, and this caused him to simply cross his fingers and hope for the best. We shared with him what we will outline in this chapter. Once he shared it with his hiring managers, the company's hiring success rate shot up to well over 85%.

Common Reasons Offers Aren't Accepted

The simple truth is, new hires are almost never really lost at the "last minute." There are red flags and subtle issues that crop up all along the way—if you're paying attention. With proper planning and strategy, you can overcome most of them to hire the candidate you really want—your first choice.

- **Family Objections.** The candidate's spouse, parents, or children strenuously object to a change.
- **Relocation Concerns.** The candidate is not comfortable with the new community, schools, recreation opportunities, social environment, etc.
- **Commute Concerns.** The candidate objects to a long daily commute between work and home.
- **Benefits Mismatch.** The hiring company's standard insurance, time off, pension/401(k), bonus structure, stock program, etc., are a step down from current levels.
- **Cost-Of-Living Differences.** The candidate would be taking an effective pay cut by accepting the offer when cost-of-living differentials between old and new community are considered.
- **The "Vision Thing."** The candidate has not bought into the vision of the hiring company or cannot see the potential benefits of leaving his present employer.

- **What Will I Be Measured Against?** The candidate will go through multiple interview rounds and never be told clearly what Success Factors they will be measured against. Without this information, a Top 5% candidate will be reluctant to move further in the process.
- **Supervisory Concerns.** The candidate and her potential supervisor in the hiring company just don't "click," or have not yet established any real rapport or trust.
- **Waiting For More Information.** The candidate is interviewing with other companies as well and is not ready to accept or reject the hiring company's offer until hearing what others may offer.
- **Hidden Agenda.** The candidate may be going through the interview process hoping to receive and accept a counteroffer.

But the number one reason offers are turned down is because **little or no discussion about the offer takes place during the interviewing process**. Everyone ignores the elephant in the room. Conventional wisdom has it that "He who brings up salary first loses," so candidates don't want to bring it up, and companies tend to have planned for a predetermined amount. Most companies usually use the predecessor's last salary amount or ballpark some percentage increase based on the incumbent's compensation. Others use a medium range of a graded compensation plan based on title.

The problem with never discussing salary and benefits during the interview process is that both the candidate and the hiring manager just hope it will all come together in the end. Worse yet, some hiring managers lowball the compensation in an offer, expecting the candidate to negotiate after the offer is presented. This is a dangerous game to play, especially if you've found a really great candidate who wasn't looking to make a change in the first place.

We've seen clients take the position that it's their game and if the candidate doesn't want to play, they'll just find someone who will. Is it any wonder why so many companies lose great candidates or can't attract them in the first place? There is a solution.

With the exception of hidden agendas, each of the above mentioned reasons for losing candidates can be worked through if you really want to hire your first choice. But you must begin to identify potential sticking points *early in the process,* and you must slowly build up to a formal offer by testing each component of the offer along the way.

Mistakes That Kill Deals

If you want to follow in the footsteps of companies with lousy batting averages, take this advice:

- **Leave The Offer Hanging.** "Here's the offer: Why don't you call me in a few days and let me know what you've decided?" We aren't kidding. A former client used to take this approach. Not surprisingly, they didn't hire as many candidates as they would have liked.
- **Specify A "Salary Range" Up Front, Then Don't Offer The Top Figure.** HR departments often ask candidates what they're making when they first arrive, and then share a potential salary range with the candidate. Unless you're prepared to offer the absolute top number to each candidate, you should not name that figure in the first place. If an HR Representative tells the candidate, "This job pays $100 to $110K," the candidate only hears "$110K." They expect to be offered the top of the range to bring them on board. Perception is everything here. The candidate perceives they are worth every penny.
- **Wait Until The Last Interview To Discuss Compensation And Benefits.** At the opposite end of the spectrum, many hiring executives don't even begin to address compensation issues until the final interview. That's far too late. You need to begin probing early. There's no sense in arriving at the end of an interview process to discover that the compensation and benefits you can offer aren't enough to bring the candidate onboard. After the second interview, when things are getting serious on both sides, the compensation discussion should begin. (More on that in a minute.)

- **Make An Inflexible Low-ball Offer.** A few thousand dollars shouldn't kill a deal—especially if the person is a Top Performer who could produce hundreds of thousands of dollars in bottom-line results for the company. Don't be a bulldog over $2,000 or even $4,000. If you've found the person who can produce the success you need, and she needs $3,000 more per year than you'd initially hoped to offer, are you really willing to let her walk away? (To be fair, when we are on a client engagement, we often have the very same discussion with candidates.) If you need to convince somebody in another department to cut open the purse strings, use the Success Factor Snapshot and focus their attention on what you believe this person will contribute to the organization.

- **Base Your Offer Solely On Their Current Compensation.** If your company's open position is a significant step up in responsibility, work hours, commute, etc., you might not be able to get away with offering your top candidate their current salary plus a couple extra thousand. Use the SFS to determine the most appropriate compensation. Especially if your top candidate is coming from a different industry or different part of the country, their current salary might not be a useful benchmark for an agreeable offer. Try to avoid pitfalls that are guided by hard-line HR policies: "We always take the candidate's current salary and add 5%—no more, no less."

- **Be A Buzzard.** When rumors circulate about a competitor who's facing hard times, being acquired, or otherwise in upheaval, call in and try to get their best people. CHEAP. Aggressive candidates will generally be willing to make a leap for very little, but Sleepers and Selective candidates will not appreciate this strategy. They know what they can accomplish, and they know what they should be earning for their work. Be prepared to step up and make it worth their while to join your firm. Otherwise, you may discover they've joined another competitor.

How To Build A Successful Offer, Step By Step

You can rarely overcome objections after an offer has been extended. It happens, yes, but we would much rather see a deal that's been carefully set up throughout the entire interview process.

Ideally, the written formal offer itself will be an anticlimax. Both parties should already know and have agreed to everything in the offer document. You don't close the deal at the end; you start closing the deal at the very first interview and continue through the second or third interviews, with a series of small "Yeses" all along the way.

Step 1: Treat every candidate who makes it through the first round of interviews as your top choice for the position. We coach our client companies to use "When…" rather than "If…" statements.

"When you come to work for us…When you're here…When you start dealing with our line-of-credit renegotiations…Your new boss…"

This language encourages candidates to visualize themselves already in the job, working for your company. It also lets them know you're seriously picturing them in the role. If you signal that you aren't just flirting but sincerely courting them, you will encourage more serious consideration on their part.

Step 2: Lay The Groundwork Early With "What If" Questions.

If you're working with a professional recruiter, they will find out a candidate's general salary and benefit expectations before the first interview. But if you're hiring for the open position yourself, you typically won't have the luxury of foreknowledge.

Your first objective, then, is to find out beginning in the first interview whether the candidate and the company are even in the same ballpark, expectation-wise. You can try the straightforward approach: "What are you making now, and what would be your expectations if you were to come on board here?" The problem with this approach is, candidates are generally reluctant to tip their hands and will reply with hazy generalities: "Well, I really hadn't thought of that, it all depends on the opportunity, there are a lot of factors to consider, blah blah blah." They've been told that he who names a number first loses, and they're trying to protect themselves.

"What If" questions, carefully and respectfully submitted, can often help to get around nebulous non-commitment. "What if, all things being equal, assuming we agree there's a good fit, we were to offer you a salary in the range of X? How would you feel about that?" (Remember, only state the highest figure in that range if you're willing to pay it.)

The "What if…how would you feel" technique is useful not only for money, but also to probe for other common objections. *"What if we were to relocate your family in January? How would you and your spouse feel about that?"*

"What if we could offer you a stock option package that would make up for some of the annual dollars in present salary we might not be able to match? How would you feel about that?"

"What if we could include a sign-on bonus that helps address the first year's compensation and include a review in six months versus one year? How would you feel about that?"

Step 3: Ask The Same Question In Different Ways. You can't overcome an objection until you know what it is. All along the way, your job is to probe and fish for *any* potential sticking points. A few questions we use are:

- Now that you've met a few people and know more about the company, what do you think?
- Where is this job right now on your list of positions you're considering? Is it #1, 2, or 3?

- How interested are you in this opportunity right now, on a scale of 1 to 10? What's turning you on or off?
- Is there anything that would keep you from accepting this position if we were to offer it to you?
- Have we addressed all the issues about your current compensation and benefits, versus what we might be able to offer you?
- Do you have enough information about the position and our company that make you feel able to make a good decision?
- Is there anything you need to know before you would be able to accept an offer?

If and when a hesitation, objection, or issue arises, work through it quickly, generously, and rationally. The value of this process is open communication. The candidate should know that you appreciate their contributions and are striving to understand and meet their needs as much as possible

Step 4: Send Up A Trial Balloon. A trial balloon isn't an actual offer. It's a prelude to an offer, a teaser. It's designed to test the candidate's openness and readiness to accept a position. It sounds like this:

"So, Cathy, we're thinking about making you an offer. Is there anything else you need to know or any concerns you have that would prevent you from accepting it?" *And then you wait.*

If the candidate hesitates, or answers in any way other than, "Great, let's hear it!" you need to take two huge steps back, find out what the issues are, and address them if possible.

"Hm. You said you were really excited about our company and the position three days ago. What's changed?" Listen carefully and tell the candidate you'll address those issues and get back to her immediately. One other useful question in such a situation is, "If we can resolve your issue about the marketing budget, would you then be in a position to accept an offer with us?"

If Cathy's response is "Yes" then you know you've covered the bases.

However, if Cathy's response is again hesitant, something else is wrong. You really need to hang in there and find out what the underlying issue is before you move forward with any offer.

If the list of issues keeps growing, the candidate likely has an agenda that probably doesn't include you. It's time to re-kindle the interviewing process with other candidates.

If, however, you are able to make adjustments, or address the candidate's misgivings, then it's time to re-test with another trial balloon.

The bottom line is this: Both parties should know what the final offer is going to be, *before it's made.*

The final test of readiness is the Start Date. After the candidate has told you she'd be excited to hear an offer, ask if she can tell you when she would be able to start. "If we were to hire you...when would you give your notice and be able to start?" Or "What if everything comes together? When do you see yourself coming to work for us?" If she can't name a specific date, that means she hasn't gotten to the point where she can "see" herself working there just yet. You haven't reached a meeting of minds.

If the candidate responds that she needs to think about it and will have to get back to you, pull out a calendar and state the date of hire that is desirable for the hiring manager and firm. Ask, "What would prevent you from giving notice to your current employer and joining our firm in two weeks?" This question will help the candidate decide and will most likely result with a definitive date.

Make The Offer An Event

Whew.

All right. You've run up the trial balloons. You've discussed all the objections and obstacles. You've tailored a package of salary and benefits that satisfies the candidate's needs and desires. You're ready to actually make the offer. What are the Do's and Don'ts?

Do make the offer for a position personally. The offer may or may not be made face-to-face, but it should be made live, at least over the phone. For executive or high-level managerial executive hires, we recommend offers be extended over a friendly meal—a business lunch or a nice dinner in a restaurant. It would even be appropriate to bring the spouse along for the event.

Do not, under any circumstances, do what one of our former clients used to do: They routinely sent out offer documents via FedEx, without even a call to tell candidate the papers were on their way. As it turned out, that's also how they terminated people; we can't recommend either practice.

Do prepare the candidate ahead of time to deal with a counter-offer. "Jim, we want your expertise here at Widgets Inc., and I'm sure your boss over at GadgetLand is going to be upset to lose you. If I were her, I'd do whatever it took to keep you. I can imagine the frustrations she'll face when she realizes she's going to have to hire and train a new person to replace you. How would you feel about being made a counteroffer? Do you feel a counteroffer would offset the fundamental reasons you and I have been discussing about why you want to join us? If she were to offer you more money, would that overcome the lack of personal growth and challenge that's been frustrating you?"

Don't make the offer into a bigger deal than it really is. Because you will not make an offer unless you're sure it will be accepted, by the time all the "What Ifs" are over, there should be very little to discuss. The offer itself should be a mere formality, like a signature on a wedding license. The entire process of making the offer and getting the candidate's signature should take two to three minutes. The rest of the dinner or phone call can be used to start talking about what's next on the horizon: the new hire's first days and weeks on the job.

Chapter Summary

❖ **Never make an offer** until you know it will be accepted.

❖ **Avoid the common mistakes** that can make deals fall apart.

❖ **Treat every candidate** as though they're your top choice.

❖ **Use "What If" questions**, followed up with "How do you feel about that…" to uncover potential sticking points.

❖ **Send up a Trial Balloon** and if the response is anything other than an enthusiastic "Great!" go back and clear up sticking points.

❖ **Prepare the candidate** for a counter-offer by telling him he'll likely face one, and reminding him of the reasons he wants to come join your company…*beyond* compensation.

Chapter 14: Transition And Follow-up

> What we've got here is a failure to communicate.
>
> *Cool Hand Luke*

Congratulations. You've just completed your first Success Factor Methodology Hire. You've got a new employee who's demonstrated the ability to do exactly what needs to be done. She's going to make a huge impact in the organization.

You've spent a lot of money and invested a lot of time in finding and hiring her. In all likelihood, you attracted her away from another company that really would have preferred to keep her.

You've compared her accomplishments to other candidates via Five-Key Question Interviews, gone through scoring with the Eight-Dimension Success Matrix form, validated her accomplishments through several Eight-Point Success Validation reference checks, run her background check, and sealed the deal with an offer that she'd been agreeing to all along. You're finished!

Wait. Not so fast.

Now is the time to make sure your new employee makes a soft landing into your organization and hits the ground running. So for a moment, let's go back to the beginning: *How can you make sure the new hire doesn't become a part of the 56% problem?*

Day One And Beyond: Assimilation Coaching

Assimilation coaching has two key components.

First, the hiring executive and their new addition must become aware of, and sensitive to, differences in work styles.

Secondly, the new hire and his manager must reach a quick understanding of Success Factors and various issues that may affect delivery.

When we work with our client companies, we recommend assimilation coaching that includes reliable assessment and debriefing on the differences in work styles between the hiring executive and their new subordinate. The new employee and the executive to whom they report must be able to understand and constructively work with each other.

Occasionally, conflicts arise not because somebody "doesn't know what they're doing," but because work styles clash.

The first few weeks and months on the job are critical, and therefore, we recommend that assessment and coaching begin on the first day a new employee starts with your company.

To help facilitate a successful transition, we recommend a third-party who is trained to administer and interpret appropriate work style assessments. There are a score of assessments, both written and Web-based, on the market that can be used in this type of coaching. The professionals with whom we work use a wide range, including the 16PF, Myers-Briggs Type Indicator (MBTI), and DISC Behavioral Assessment. The categories below are just some of the common dimensions in which dramatic differences can cause the 56% problem.

- **Extraversion vs. Introversion.** *Extraverts* tend to talk fast and think later. Often, they don't know what they will say until they say it. They enjoy going to meetings and tend to let their opinion be heard. They feel frustrated if they are not given the opportunity to state their viewpoint. *Introverts*, on the other hand, rehearse things before saying them out loud in front of a group. They often say, "Let me think about that for a while." They enjoy peace and quiet. They are generally perceived as good listeners. An extraverted boss can become frustrated when an introverted employee doesn't have the right answer instantly or doesn't speak up in meetings. At the same time, introverted bosses can become frustrated when extraverted employees drop by for "trivial" chatter, or break concentration with every random thought that seems to pop into their head.

- **Analytic vs. Intuitive Thinking.** *Analytic thinkers* move to a conclusion by following a set, precise, logical pattern. *A* leads to *B*, *B* leads to *C*, *C* leads to *D*. *Intuitive thinkers*, on the other hand, sometimes leap directly from *A* to *E* without all the "extra" steps in between. Intuitives frustrate Analytics by "skipping over" details that are important to them; Analytics frustrate Intuitives who can't understand why somebody needs to be walked through *all* the steps that, to them, are obvious "givens." In general, Intuitives tend to be the visionaries and innovators who can conceive great things, while Analytics are the detail-oriented folks who can actually take those grand visions, break them down into logical processes, and make them work.

- **Dominance vs. Compliance.** Some people are simply more likely to be aggressive, or dominant, while others are more likely to be compliant and cooperative. There can be several sources of conflict when either extreme blossoms in the workplace. Highly dominant people can unthinkingly railroad their subordinates (and even supervisors), while highly compliant people might not speak up when they see flaws in a plan, just to "keep the peace." The first anybody hears about their dissatisfaction is the day they turn in their resignation.

- **Thinkers vs. Feelers.** Thinkers value logic, reason, facts, and analysis, with very little need for pats on the back and "attaboys." Feelers value emotion, community, and benevolence, and often have a greater need for demonstrative approval from supervisors. Frustration sets in when a Feeler completes a project and the Thinker doesn't acknowledge the effort the Feeler puts in. Over time, the Feeler begins to question whether the Thinker values the work that is being done. Ultimately, a Top Talent Feeler may well quit because he or she didn't receive recognition.

- **Independence vs. Dependence.** Independent personalities neither need nor want involvement from others when they have a job to do. As bosses, they expect to be able to hand off a project or a task and trust subordinates to figure it out themselves. As employees, they expect to be given an assignment and then left alone while they do the work. Dependent personalities, on the other hand, need closer day-to-day interactions with team members to feel comfortable. As supervisors, they check in more often with their direct reports (sometimes going so far as to micro-manage), and as employees, they tend to reconfirm, raise questions, apprise of status, and double-check with their boss as they complete a project.

A good third party professional, armed with accurate assessments, can help the hiring executive and their new hire recognize their inherent differences before they've caused any friction. Forewarned is forearmed.

Some of our clients extend this process of assessing work style differences to the team level. In the first week, a new hire and his or her team need to hear, "Congratulations. You're all smart, accomplished people, and here are some of the ways you might find you have trouble with each other a few months down the road." This can go a long way toward heading off potential conflict at the pass, and in many cases can help to improve the workings of *all* members of a team—not just the newest addition.

If toes get stepped on too hard during the first dance, people may never regain their balance. We can't stress enough the importance of communication and work style coaching to help ease the transition from one culture to another.

Finally, having traveled in a full circle, here we are—back to the beginning. Expectations.

By the time the new hire arrives, it's possible that some conditions that existed when the hiring team wrote the Success Factor Snapshot have changed. During the first week, it is important to communicate the changes and reasons involved, then revisit the Snapshot, revise it where necessary, clarify expectations, answer any new questions, and brief the new hire on any changes in resources or capabilities that might impact the situation, obstacles, or goals.

Now it's time to turn the SFS into a living document. On a monthly basis, the hiring executive should conduct "one-on-ones" with the new hire. Focusing these monthly discussions around the SFS provides the hiring executive with a tool to manage flawless execution and ensure that the Success Factors are achieved. Using the SFS as the core in these discussions provides a framework of objectivity for constructive feedback and coaching. Again, nobody should have to wait a year before they hear, "Things aren't working out." The Success Factor Snapshot should be reviewed and revised as necessary when the Success Factors are accomplished, priorities change, and new business issues surface. It forms the backbone of the first-year performance review. If it's used as a hub for your managerial processes, it can become a living document that guides every person in the company toward the common goals and successes that will ensure the company prospers.

Chapter Summary

❖ **The First Week is a critical transitional period** for new employees, and missteps early on may never be remedied.

❖ **Transition coaching** based on personality traits, preferences, and attitudes can help to inform the entire team of potential sticking points before problems develop.

❖ **The Success Factor Snapshot continues to play a role** even after a new hire comes on board. Revisiting expectations during the first week can help avert unpleasant surprises further down the line.

❖ **The Success Factor Snapshot becomes a living document** providing the hiring executive with a performance management tool and vehicle for one-to-one coaching.

SECTION 5: THE PROCESS IN ACTION

Chapter 15: Eight Steps To Top Talent

This book was written to help you make better hiring decisions that lead to more successful hires. We have shared with you, in these chapters, all of the tools and tips we use with our corporate clients on a daily basis.

You can take everything we've written here and apply it directly to your own business. It takes discipline, drive, tenacity, and the willingness to make it happen, no matter what.

We won't lie to you; it's not easy. The Success Factor Methodology is a fundamental rethinking of many ingrained hiring practices and poor interviewing habits. And while breaking bad habits takes hard work, it is possible.

When it comes to executive and managerial searches, we fully understand that every search firm will claim to cover the steps outlined in this book. We want to reinforce one message: Make sure their focus is on *results, expectations,* and *outcomes,* as opposed to merely tinkering with your old job description, then pulling a few candidates from their firm's database.

When you are in the process of a high-impact hire, we encourage you to focus on value. Every search firm should present and manage a systematic, valid, and reliable hiring process that will generate a sizeable pool of candidates who are capable of delivering the results you expect.

Hold your search firm responsible. They should deliver value, service, and insights every step of the way.

Companies that hire us generally don't have the time, focus, or energy to implement the Success Factor Methodology on their own.

As we outline the eight steps below, keep in mind that these passages describe how we manage the process on retained search assignments. The execution would differ in some steps if the hiring executive managed the process alone, without us.

Step 1: Build The Success Factor Snapshot

When we begin a retained search assignment, we go to the client and begin the process of extracting vital information. We gather everybody who is involved in the hiring process in the same room. The Success Factor Methodology is only as good as the team's weakest link, so we ask that every stakeholder be present for the kickoff meeting. (If all members can't be present, we insist that they participate in approving the finished Success Factor Snapshot before we actively begin to solicit candidates). Without early buy-in by all stakeholders, there is always a risk of having to start over again sixty or ninety days down the road.

During Step 1, the consensus building begins. We brief the team on the Success Factor Methodology, explaining the rationale and the evidence behind our system, and then establish buy-in among all involved parties. Only at that point do we begin identifying the major goals for the position to be filled.

Most first meetings are time-consuming, draining, and even a bit awkward, because the hiring executives often are not used to thinking about tying individual performance directly into the company's operating plan.

One of the most remarkable observations we make during Step 1 is that often, the assembled hiring team has never thought about linking a position's expected results with departmental goals (and ultimately the corporate goals). When we ask the hiring team to name the main goal for the open position, the response tends to be vague, with no specifications for results or accountability.

We've had first meetings in which it became apparent that, while the company initially *thought* they wanted a Sales Director, the expectations they were outlining really defined a Marketing Vice President. It happens in reverse as well; one $50M company called us in because they "needed a CFO." By the end of our Step 1 meeting, they realized that what they really needed was a solid Controller.

Sometimes Step 1 takes more than one meeting. It nearly always takes several hours of discussion and clarification to reach consensus and completion.

Step 2: Plan Collaborative Sourcing Strategy

In Step 2, we partner with our client to brainstorm where their ideal candidates are likely employed, how we can reach them, and what will attract them to the open position.

A key outcome of this step is a compelling marketing statement—a distinctive, attention-grabbing statement that will appeal to and energize Selective and Sleeper candidates.

We can help clients troubleshoot early in Step 2 to determine whether the initial sourcing plan is likely to reach too wide or too narrow a candidate pool. For example, they may be erroneously focusing only within their own specific industry, when in fact the leadership they require may need to come from outside their comfort zone. Sometimes a true outside perspective is needed to bring about dramatic change or reinvigorate a stagnant business.

The end result of Step 2 is a thorough sourcing plan that identifies specific channels we should target (in addition to our own proprietary databases) to locate Selective and Sleeper candidates. These may include industry networking channels, trade conferences, best practices organizations, trade magazines and collateral, directories, specific companies, and so on.

A word to the wise: *You don't need a recruiter to find Aggressive candidates.* Aggressive candidates will always be available, sending their resumes in to HR. You only need a recruiter if you want to make sure you're including as many Selective and Sleeper candidates as possible in your candidate pool.

Step 3: Identify And Verify Success Prospects

Unlike most executive search firms, we do not hit prospective job candidates hard at the beginning with a generic sales pitch.

We *never* kick off a sourcing call to a candidate by saying, "Wow, do we have a great opportunity for you! It pays X. It's with a fantastic company that is looking for Y. You're perfect for the job! Send me your resume right away."

We won't do that, because a hard sales approach *doesn't work* when you're speaking with top talent Selective and Sleeper candidates. In fact, nothing will close the door to further communication faster than pushing too hard at the beginning.

We initiate the call instead by using the suggestive power of "What If" with every candidate. Truly top-notch candidates are always open to the possibility of becoming and doing more—that's what makes them who they are and one of the best.

Our questions might be, "What if we could present you with an opportunity that provided an outlet for you to better use your creativity?" Or, "What would you do if our client allowed you to effect a change that satisfied your career objectives for the next three years?" Or, "What would an attractive opportunity look like if you were to consider making a move?"

The "What If" approach is an invitation to start a dialogue that will zero in on a potential Sleeper candidate's motivation to make a move. It is not uncommon for Selective and Sleeper candidates to say, "I'm happy and not interested" three or four times before they finally become interested. Persistence and a professional approach opens these uniquely qualified candidates up to a serious dialogue and potential presentation to our clients.

In-depth phone screening of promising candidates often takes more than one call. We generally conduct at least two. Early in the search, the phone screening addresses the basics (the candidate's accomplishments in their current position). If the candidate doesn't get a passing grade here, they are not moved into the pool of potential candidates.

Many times, these early conversations uncover nuggets of information that the hiring company might not get without a thorough phone screen.

Candidates often tell us they thought our phone screen was the end of our interviewing process because it was so lengthy. But the next step is an in-depth, face-to-face interview with us. It is here that we practice what we preach. We cover all five key questions and put the candidates under the microscope. This interview may take another two hours for top candidates.

It should have been a recruiter who coined the phrase, "many are called but few are chosen." It is not uncommon for us to speak with 150 potential candidates for any given search. Our phone screen will whittle that down to 20 or 30 potential candidates and the one-on-one interviews will then identify the four or five top candidates that will actually be presented to our client.

During one of our searches, one of our clients nearly lost the person they ended up hiring. They were surprised to see the name of a candidate they had actually "screened out" (based on his resume alone) among the four top candidates we presented to them.

"We've already seen this candidate's resume," the client told us on the phone. "We passed on him. Let's not talk to him."

"Really? You took a pass?"

"Yes."

"Well, based on our interviews, we really believe strongly that you should reconsider and give him a chance. In fact, we think he's the person you're going to end up hiring."

Resistance was fairly significant, but because we had conducted a thorough interview, we were able to demonstrate the candidate's ability to deliver the expected results. We knew what he had to offer, and we knew what the company needed based on the Success Factor Snapshot. We were persistent and insisted they allow the candidate to be interviewed based on the candidate's successful track record of accomplishments relative to the SFS.

Not surprisingly (at least to us), the company did end up offering that particular candidate the position.

This story drives home the true value that a professional executive recruiter can bring to the table early in the game, even before the first face-to-face encounters occur. (As a postscript, six months after that employee was hired, he had already been promoted. Needless to say, our client was thrilled.)

The average amount of time we've spent with each candidate by the time we present the finalists for consideration is between four and five hours, including a 45-minute research interview, two full preliminary phone interviews, and a face-to-face meeting.

As a result, in the past twenty years, we have *never once* had a client tell us, "That candidate was not qualified to be here interviewing for this position." We take that record seriously and we are proud of it.

Step 4: Create Candidate Success Profiles

After preliminary phone interviews and a face-to-face interview with candidates, we complete the Eight-Dimension Success Matrix form for each candidate who will be presented to the client.

We pre-rank them according to how well they meet the criteria spelled out in the SFS, and we bundle the Matrix with any supporting documentation. These success profiles are delivered to the client company and become the foundation of assessment.

These success profiles are a wonderful opportunity to call the attention of the hiring team to particular issues, highlights, strengths, and potential sticking points.

Step 5: Coordinate Success Factor Interviews

When the interviews themselves are scheduled, depending on client resources and the level of involvement they would like from us, we may do any—or all—of the following to facilitate the process:

- Coach clients about the importance of a positive first impression and pleasant interviewing experience for the candidate.
- Sit with the interviewing team ahead of time to help direct discussion and development of structured interview questions.
- Sit in on interviews and model the magnifying-glass approach technique.
- Help keep the interview team focused on the Five Key Questions that are clearly job-related and directly linked to the Success Factor Snapshot.
- Guide development of homework assignments for the final candidate.
- Stress the importance of internal enforcement for consistent completion of the Eight-Dimension Success Matrix form by all interviewers and ensure meeting of the minds regarding consensus.
- Facilitate group discussion and debriefing after a day of interviewing.
- Coach the hiring executive on how to describe and present the position and company in an enticing, exciting way.
- Work with the team after each round of interviews to identify any remaining gaps that should be discovered in subsequent rounds and develop a plan to address these issues.
- Ensure the SFS is appropriately used to manage candidate's performance in conjunction with the company objectives.

We've been told—by clients—that some executive recruiters "dump and disappear," dropping a chunk of paperwork on the desk of the executive who retained them and then leaving the client to his or her own devices.

Our approach is different. We want to be trusted advisors, like CPAs and attorneys. We actively seek out involvement in the interview process and conduct follow up discussions to provide guidance after-the-fact. The more we share our accumulated knowledge and help guide our client through the process, the better the outcome and the better our clients feel about using the Success Factor Methodology.

Once a client has narrowed the selection down to the top one or two candidates, it's time to validate the information collected during the interview process. We conduct extensive reference checks using our Eight-Point Success Validation Form. In addition, we also facilitate in-depth background checks, and, if necessary work style assessments through third parties.

Step 6: Overcome Obstacles To Hire

From day one, beginning with the first phone interviews, our methodology allows us to address potential obstacles to hiring top talent. By the time the offer is made, there should be no surprises left to break the deal unexpectedly.

Too often in hiring situations, questions are not asked until it is too late in the process to deal effectively with them. Knowing what to ask and when to ask is critical to heading off any sticking points. In many instances, a candidate's active withdrawal is subtle—the candidate stops returning calls, delays scheduling interviews, or is not as forthcoming as he was at the beginning of the process. These are all signs of a problem. Our expertise and years of experience with these subtle signs in the process is just one reason for our successful track record. As a result, we can identify and resolve candidate issues before they've decided to back off or completely exclude themselves from the process.

Beginning with the end in mind, we use "what if" to bring about a meeting of the minds on everything from the scope of the job, compensation, the benefits package, cost of living differentials, lifestyle tradeoffs, and relocation issues.

Preparing the candidate for a potential counteroffer and having in-depth discussions about how they will respond to a counteroffer is something companies rarely do, but we start addressing that issue at the beginning of the process. Because we only work with top talent, we always expect a counteroffer.

On the rare occasion that the client's top choice gets "cold feet," we also have the objectivity, as outsiders, to deal with those issues and intercede as a third party who can act as a career coach, helping to clarify and reinforce what excited the candidate about the opportunity in the first place.

Step 7: Facilitate Compensation And Benefits Negotiation

Our position as a third party is especially valuable in final salary and benefits negotiations. We believe one of the biggest problems is that too often compensation is either never discussed, or at best, out of six hours of interviewing, salary discussion gets one or two minutes. Superficial discussion only creates numerous problems when candidate selection nears completion. Our clients and candidates know exactly what the compensation issues are long before an offer is made.

Discussion up front ensures the company does not waste time interviewing candidates who aren't an appropriate fit, or leading candidates down a path that leads to major disappointment. By managing compensation issues during each step of the interviewing process, we help our clients ensure they will not make an offer that is turned down.

Step 8: Transition And Follow-up

Finally, once the deal is inked and the candidate is wrapping up loose ends at his or her former company, we continue to work with our client to be sure the new hire's critical first 100 days are as smooth and productive as possible. We stay in touch with our candidate between acceptance of offer and start date, and if the client desires, we work to arrange necessary transition assessment and communication coaching.

The bottom line is that when we complete a search, we are 100% comfortable that the new employee will be capable of delivering the expectations identified in the SFS and he or she will become a valuable and profitable addition to our client's team for years to come.

We can back each of our searches with 100% guarantee. We believe the end of a successful search is not an ending, but a beginning. We stay in contact with our client and candidates in an effort to follow the story as it unfolds over the years.

Our searches result in key executive hires that persist for years— even decades. We believe that's the way it should be.

And Beyond...

We hope you will take to heart what you've learned in this book and apply it in your own organization. If you have suggestions, questions, or feedback, please do not hesitate to contact us at authors@impacthiringsolutions.com.

Please accept our best wishes for your success in the years to come, and our thanks for your attention. The Success Factor Methodology works, and we sincerely believe it will help you and your organization to hire more effectively. Use it completely. Use it consistently. With a little effort, every interview is an opportunity for you to become a better hiring executive and an opportunity for you to greatly impact the future of your company.

SECTION 6: APPENDIXES

Appendix 1: A Recent Hiring Best-Practices Bibliography

Anonymous. "Recruiters Face More Obstacles in Convincing Candidates to Move." *Executive Search Review* Sept. 2003 <http://www.hunt-scanlon.com/newsletters/search.htm>. This article discusses how recruiters are having trouble wooing top candidates to new positions, which they attribute to the sluggish economy. The recruiters they interviewed noted that the candidates are requiring more information up front, including very specific job descriptions and relocation concerns. They found that companies that were unwilling to fully examine the ramifications of the switch for the job candidate will find that candidate is unwilling to take a chance with them.

Anonymous. "Understanding Failure." *Across The Board* July/Aug. 2003: 27.
Interview with the authors of two books about executive failure, Sydney Finkelstein (*Why Smart Executives Fail*) and David Dotlich (*Why CEOs Fail*). The interview discusses the difference in philosophy between their two books, recent executive failure examples and what makes a bad leader.

Andersson, Don. "Avoid Executive Failure Traps." *Executive Excellence* July 1999: 16.
The article cites the findings of several studies: 35% of all executives entering new positions will fail; 40% of all executives entering new positions will either leave voluntarily, be terminated, or receive an unsatisfactory review within 18 months; and the typical Fortune 500 company has had 2.3 CEOs in the last decade. The author suggests that companies must address four "fit factors" to prevent executive failure. The first is Position Alignment, which includes adjusting the

job descriptions and mission statements; developing a clear Corporate Culture and interviewing with this in mind; clearly stating and prioritizing Expectations from the start; and if Change is crucial to the position, provide the executive with a "change coach" to help the transitions.

Association of Executive Search Consultants. "Executive Resume Poll." April 2004 <http://www.aesc.org>.

> A survey of 538 senior executives found that 78% find that the most important resume components—objective/mission and results/accomplishments—are the hardest to successfully convey. Peter Felix, AESC President noted that, "Reducing your life's work to a resume is a daunting task for many executives. Some underscore the impact of their role. Others inflate it."

Association of Executive Search Consultants. "Underutilized Executive Skills Poll." March 2004 <http://www.aesc.org>.

> A poll of 693 senior executives found that 43% say their management and leadership skills are under-utilized. Peter Felix, AESC President said "This is clearly a call for corporate executives to rethink whether they are getting the best out of their senior executives—and whether they have the right person in the right role."

Boren, Susan S., and Heidrick, Robert L. "Get serious to make CEO evaluations work." *Spencer Stuart Governance Letter* 2004: 54-56. <http://www.spencerstuart.com>.

> This white paper from executive search firm Spencer Stuart discusses the process of CEO evaluations, which the board of directors must formally conduct. Though they found 72% of companies they surveyed had a CEO evaluation system in place, they have found through their work that most companies are very informal about it. However, the authors feel it is essential to develop a structured process that will benefit the CEO and the entire company. The guidelines they suggest include establishing the format ahead of time,

agreeing on what is being measured, have the CEO perform a self-evaluation and survey and interview managers and others throughout the company. These evaluations will then help establish the state of the company and develop a better relationship between the board and the top executive.

Cairo, Peter C., and Dotlich, David L. *Why CEOs Fail: The 11 Behaviors That Can Derail Your Climb to the Top and How to Manage Them.* Indianapolis: Jossey-Bass, 2003.

The authors lay out a series of "derailers" that can lead to executive downfall. These are: Arrogance: You think that you're right, and everyone else is wrong; Melodrama: You need to be the center of attention; Volatility: you're subject to mood swings; Excessive Caution: You're afraid to make decisions; Habitual Distrust: You focus on the negatives; Aloofness: You're disengaged and disconnected; Mischievousness: You believe that rules are made to be broken; Eccentricity: You try to be different just for the sake of it; Passive Resistance: What you say is not what you really believe; Perfectionism: You get the little things right and the big things wrong; Eagerness to Please: You try to win the popularity contest. The authors alternate high profile cases (the arrogance of Enron CEO Jeff Skilling, the melodrama of Vivendi Universals' Jean-Marie Messier, Rick Thoman's aloofness at Xerox) with compelling case examples from their coaching practice.

Center for Advanced Human Resource Studies. "Waging the War for Talent." *HR Spectrum* Sept.-Oct. 1999: 1, 4, 6.

Discusses the difficulty large corporations have recruiting and retaining top talent. This was written during the dot-com boom, when start-up companies were attracting people with stock options. They also found that there is an increase in job mobility, with most people only changing jobs once or twice in a career in the beginning of the decade but that number has jumped to five times by 1999. The article discusses the benefits and costs of performance-based pay programs, which are more expensive to implement and operate, yet help to retain top talent who feel they should be compensated for their better performance. They conclude that this type of system is most beneficial when the top performers contribute to the company significantly more than lower performers. Otherwise their benefit to the company does not outweigh the cost of the system.

Charan, Ram. "Ending the CEO Succession Crisis." *Harvard Business Review* Feb. 2005: 72.

The author discusses the typical problems associated with executive succession. He cites the study by the Corporate Leadership Council, which surveyed 276 large companies and found that only 20% of responding HR executives were satisfied with their top-management succession processes. After discussing the various issues with selecting an external or internal candidate and why executive searches often fail, Charan uses the succession strategy of Colgate-Palmolive to illustrate the best way to groom candidates long before the company ever needs them to step into the top spot.

Charan, Ram and Colvin, Geoffery. "Why CEOs Fail" *Fortune* 21 June 1999: 68.

The authors estimate that 70% of executive failures are due to bad execution of strategies. A major part of this is their inability to put the right people into the right jobs and the related issue of not fixing people problems quickly. The authors account this to a lack of emotional strength or failure to focus on the people in the organization. They relate examples of failures and successes in major companies such as GE, IBM, and Delta.

Christian & Timbers. "Trends in Executive Suite: COOs Train and Transition for the CEO Position." 2004 <http://www.ctnet.com>.

The author looks at the trend to hire a Chief Operation Officer to groom for the CEO position. Rather than taking chances with a slightly green CEO, the COO to CEO succession plan allows for acclimation to the company culture and inner workings before taking over. They have found in most cases, the COO moves to the CEO position within six to twelve months.

Ciampa, Dan. "Almost Ready: How Leaders Move Up." *Harvard Business Review* Jan. 2005: 46.

This article discusses the pitfalls of finding replacement CEOs. Ciampa notes that although many managers are put on the track to be put in the top position, many never make it due to their focus on the wrong issues. He identifies several categories of necessary capabilities, such as managing the political environment and personal style that separate the merely good CEO candidate from the elite one that will actually make it to the top spot. He illustrates his points with "anonymous" examples of different people in the number two position who either never made it to the top or were wrongly placed there before they were ready.

Corcodilos, Nick. "Death By Lethal Reputation: The Demise of An Employer." <http://www.asktheheadhunter.com>.

This white paper enumerates the fatal mistakes that can be made during the hiring process to scare off top-level candidates forever. Essentially, companies need to treat their candidates with respect—have them interviewed by knowledgeable managers, not low-level personnel employees; make them feel welcome and appreciated because they took valuable time off work to meet with you; don't allow cynicism and indifference to poison the well of new employees. The author centers his paper around an unnamed Silicon Valley software company that, despite its prestige, could not entice top-level candidates to return for second interviews because of these fatal errors.

Deal, Jennifer J., Sessa, Valerie I., and Taylor, Jodi J. "Choosing Executives: A Research Report on Peak Selection Simulation." Center for Creative Leadership Press, 1999.

>Hypothesizing that the CEO selection process is inadequate, CCL researchers used the Peak Selection Simulation to ask 621 decision-makers specific questions about how they use interviews, HR information, and search firm reports to select top-level candidates. This report, containing thirty figures and tables and a comprehensive reference list, documents this research and provides useful insights that can lead to better selection outcomes.

Finkelstein, Sydney. *Why Smart Executives Fail: And What You Can Learn From Their Mistakes.* Portfolio, 2003.

>Finkelstein, a professor of strategy and leadership at Dartmouth's Tuck School of Business, based his study on interviews with 200 executives. The book explores the core causes for failure and finds, surprisingly, that "neither ineptitude nor greed are among them." The book relates the stories of great business disasters and demonstrates that there are specific, identifiable ways in which many businesses regularly make themselves vulnerable to failure. Finkelstein found that a major theme that came out of the research was that executives at these companies knew exactly what was going on, yet they chose not to act on the facts and information they had. Part of it is the cultural dimension, but the author also describes a strategic dimension, leadership issues, and organizational breakdowns, which he refers to as "business-school logic gone bad."

Global Consulting Partnership. "Executive Coaching: An Investment In Creating Masterful Leadership." *Executive Coaching* 2000. <http://www.tgcpinc.com/tgcp.html>.

>This white paper explores the importance of executive coaching. It lays out six leadership roles that an executive

must take on to be fully effective: the explorer, forging vision and change; the beacon, instilling trust and inspiring commitment to the vision; the advocate, the clearest voice in support of visionary, strategic, value-driven behavior; the facilitator, creating a consultative work style; the partner, encouraging a supportive and collaborative work style; and the coach, bring out the best in the organization's people. For those executives not up to snuff in all these areas, executive coaching could be the best solution. They claim that top executives are aggressive learners, but only 10% of people are naturally active learners. However, they believe that the skills can be taught. These include mental agility, interpersonal finesse, mastery of change, and goal orientation

.

Global Consulting Partnership. "Executive Development and Succession Planning." 2000 <http://www.tgcpinc.com/tgcp.html>.
This white paper presents a clear process for succession planning. It lays out the objectives of taking inventory of key managerial candidates in terms of leadership styles, skills, gaps and ultimate potential, and designing an advancement plan for each candidate that is incorporated into their performance process. It suggests reviewing current job descriptions and updating as necessary, then including key leadership competencies into these and building a job profile that measures the need for each success factor. They recommend testing all candidates for the five key predictors of future success: intellect, conscientiousness, urgency, emotional stability, and agreeableness. In addition, having co-workers and supervisors at the company evaluate the candidate gives a more well-rounded perception of their leadership style and skills. In the end, candidates that show strong potential should have development opportunities built into their advancement plan.

Grossman, Robert J. "Forging a Partnership – Executive Turnover."
HR Magazine April 2003.

> This article discusses the role of the HR executive during
> periods of executive transition. The author feels it is essential
> for the HR executive to assist the new CEO in hitting the
> ground running at the corporation. They should be prepared
> to give very specific feedback and information regarding
> the employees, including current satisfaction surveys,
> compensation and benefit analysis and plans to increase their
> reputation as an employer. The author provides various tips
> on developing a good rapport with the CEO not only to help
> the executive transition, but to be sure the HR executive
> retains their own position.

Hornberger Management Company. "Construction Executive
Retention Survey." 2003 <http://www.hmc.com>.

> Their survey includes findings from surveying executives in
> the construction industry. They found many CEOs believe
> they should spend 30% to 40% of their time finding and
> developing leaders, yet only 15% felt they were performing
> this role. In addition, the executives felt that former number
> twos typically don't make great CEOs. Many CEOs do
> not have subordinates who are stronger or better than
> they were when they were in a number two position. Over
> 65% of CEOs who are promoted internally fail to meet
> owner's expectations for growth and lose market share. This
> contradicts the trend of grooming COOs for taking over the
> CEO position in the future that was discussed in Christian
> and Timber's white paper.

Joiner, Harry. "How To Identify A Problem Solver." *6 Figure Jobs.com
E-Newsletter* Sept. 2004. <http://www.6figurejobs.com>.

> The author notes that most of his clients are seeking
> problem solvers in their executive searches. To find them,
> he enumerates seven steps to successful problem solving
> that the interviewer can walk the candidate through while
> describing a problem they solved in a previous job. First they

must define the problem, including the cause and effect. Then the candidate should define the objectives they wanted to achieve by solving the problem. They should then discuss the alternatives they generated and next recap their detailed action plan. The interviewer should then have the candidate go over the worst-case scenarios that could have occurred with his plan. Next, they should discuss the communication of the plan, who it affected, and whether they were properly informed. Finally, have the candidate address how the plan was implemented and the consequences of failing to meet any part of the plan. The author notes that really examining how the candidate solved problems in the past will help reveal how they will solve them in the future. If they candidate is not challenged in the interview process the company could pay a hefty price in the future.

Lewis, Diane. "Top Firms Enlisting Coaches For New Execs Practice Intended to Smooth Transition, Increase Retention." *The Boston Globe* 9 Mar. 2003: G1.

This article examines the trend of hiring assimilation coaches for new executives since studies have shown that there is a high failure rate within the first few years. This service is often provided by the executive search firms that placed the executive, functioning as a guarantee of their work. Other executives are hiring coaches for themselves to assist them in their crucial first hundred days. The author gave examples of new executives who established themselves early with the help of coaches.

Lucier, Chuck, Schuyt, Rob and Spiegel, Eric. "Why CEOs Fall–The Causes and Consequences of Turnover at the Top." *Booz Allen Hamilton Special Report* May 2003. <http://extfile.bah.com/livelink/livelink/110173/?func=doc.Fetch&nodeid=110173>.

This comprehensive study of departing CEOs from the world's 2,500 largest publicly traded companies of 1995, 1998, 2000, and 2001, analyzes the personal demographic information of departing CEOs and the financial performance of their companies. They have found that the rate of CEO changes due to performance has increased by 130 percent between 1995 and 2001 (an update of the study for 2002 has shown that rate to be closer to 300 percent). Their findings also show that the tenure for CEOs is declining, going down 23% between 1995 and 2001. They conclude that if a CEO wants to extend his career in this changing environment he must 1) Deliver acceptable and consistent total returns to shareholder; 2) Manage against the major risk factors to rapidly adapt to changes in the market; and 3) Define and achieve their agenda quickly. The study provides statistics sorted by industries and regions regarding ages of ascension, average tenures, and reasons for leaving the CEO position.

Mendels, Pamela. "Gone But Not Forgotten." *Business Week* June 2001.
This article discusses the trend of "assimilation" counseling for executives who have been let go. This service allows for outside coaching for the first 100 days in the executives new position. The coaching often helps avoid the mistakes that may have caused the problems in their last position since it requires the executive to examine themselves with the aid of outside perspective.

Paese, Matthew J. "Growing Your Own Leaders: The 'Acceleration' Center." *Development Dimensions International* <http://www.ddiworld.com>.
This article points out the need for "growing" talent from within an organization due to the shortage of executive talent. However, they feel that succession management systems generally fail because they stop after the identification of potential, without moving onto development of their talent. The author identifies to faulty assumptions that lead to problems: 1) that identifying acceleration pool members is sufficient to improve leadership depth and 2) the identification process provides sufficient information

to launch individual accelerated development plans. Very specific assessment of individuals is needed to pinpoint which areas need development, then a plan must be implemented to improve these individual needs. The concept of an Acceleration Center is described as a flight simulator for executives, using outside assessors and technology to test and develop the potential leader's skills.

Parker, Brian. "Construction Executive Hiring Permanently Changes After War." *Construction Executive A/E/C Newswire* 15 Apr. 2003 <http://www.constructionexecutive.com>.
A survey of 229 construction CEOs and 286 construction executives found that since 9/11 a greater emphasis has been placed on candidate screening for executive hiring (including the increased demand for third-party reference checking, detailed background checks, assessment testing, fee-based company research, and probationary hires). The executives felt that probationary hiring was a significant improvement, because it demanded accountability for the first 90 days of the job, which led to a better rate of retention among newly hired executives.

Recruiters Network. "Creating the Perfect Candidate Interviewing Experience From Concept to Reality." *6 Figure Jobs.com E-Newsletter* July 2004. <http://www.6figurejobs.com>.
The article points out that job candidates should be treated like respected and valued customers so that they leave with a favorable impression of the company. They suggest incorporating several ideas into interviewing methodology, such as providing very detailed information on how to arrive at the interview on time, beginning the interview on time and apologizing if things are running late, as well as providing all interviewers with a copy of the position profile, the candidate's resume, and the interviewing schedule. Each interviewer should also end the session by asking if the candidate has any questions and providing a specific time to get back to them with additional information if that is

needed. If the interview is running overtime, be sure to ask the candidate's permission since they could have another appointment scheduled. The article feels that applying these simple suggestions will yield better results in the recruiting efforts.

RHR International. "Hitting the Ground Running: Accelerating Executive Integration." *Executive Research* Sept. 2002. <http://www.rhrinternational.com>.

> The research consisted of both an online survey and in-depth interviews with over 100 participants from Canada and the United States. Multiple industries and functions were represented. Participants ranged from senior-level managers to CEOs. Included were newly hired executives, long-term employees, human resource representatives, search consultants and executive coaches. They note that 51% of those surveyed felt that integration takes longer than they expect, since though most hoped it would take 6 months, the reality was between 9 and 18 months. Their research suggests that there are three essential components for a successful integration: clearly defining the role, developing strategic relationships and learning about and adapting to the culture of the organization. Without attention to all these components the new executive will likely fail. The study found that companies often do little to assist the integration process, so it is often up to the new executive, since 72% of survey participants were satisfied with their own efforts to integrate, only 39% were satisfied with their organization's efforts to integrate them. They give companies suggestions on how to best assist the integration process, because the more they contribute the faster the new CEO will be fully incorporated into the organization.

Rock, Michael E. "Avoiding Costly Hiring Mistakes." *Six Figure Jobs.com E-Newsletter* Jan. 2003. <http://www.6figurejobs.com>.

> The author stressed the importance of EQ (emotional quotient) in the workplace. The term EQ was coined by the clinical psychologist Dr. Reuven Bar-On and the author cites

the findings of his work with acculturation rates for Hispanic immigrants. A high EQ is an indicator of clear thinking, healthy emotions, and appropriate actions, all of which are essential for a good employee. Therefore, the author feels that the emotional factors should be integrated into the hiring process to help identify the "soft skills" that are essential to capable employees.

Rubin, Debra K. "Executive Recruiters Are More Than Boardroom Brokers." *Engineering News-Record* 22 Dec. 2003: 22.

No group in engineering and construction is probably more misunderstood, mistrusted, and misused than executive recruiters. In many firms, executive hiring has long been an informal thing, similar to the handshake deals among partners and clients that pepper the self-described "good ol' boy industry." In its just-released annual survey of more than 1,000 contractor executives, search firm Hornberger Management Co., Wilmington, Delaware, reports that 69% say their firms are short on talent and 66% say they do not do enough to attract the people they need. While industry observers say executive pay and bonuses took a hit in 2003, regulators are still watching how total compensation packages are developed, including signing bonuses, housing allowances, interest-free loans, and stock options.

Sessa, Valerie I., and Taylor, Jodi J. *Executive Selection: Strategies for Success*. Indianapolis: Jossey-Bass Publishers, 2000.

Recent crises in several executive suites demonstrate that a single misstep in selecting top executives can spell trouble for even the most stable of organizations. Yet the development of clear criteria for executive selection is too often pushed aside in the face of more immediate challenges. Based on Center for Creative Leadership research and the authors' extensive experience in dealing with top-level executives, this book outlines a comprehensive system for matching the right person with the right job.

Strauss, Gary. "Troubled Firms Entice CEOs With Platinum Pay." *USA Today* 21 Feb. 2003: 1B.

> This article examines the executive compensation packages that are growing to huge numbers in recent months. Median CEO compensation was $10.2 million at big companies in 2002, and the increasing payouts will likely expand this across the board. The article uses specific examples of companies who have recently used this "golden hello" to entice new executives and the past results that show that a big paycheck does not necessary guarantee good performance.

Watkins, Michael. *The First 90 Days: Critical Success Strategies For New Leaders At All Levels.* Cambridge: Harvard Business School Press, 2003.

> Watkins, an associate professor of Business Administration at Harvard Business School, discusses the need for new executives to quickly reach, what he calls, the "break-even point" where new leaders have contributed as much value to the corporation as they have taken from it. He provides a blueprint for addressing the challenges of personal transition and company transformation that is crucial to the first few months on the job.

Appendix 2: Downloads

You may visit our Web site, www.impacthiringsolutions.com, to download the following items. You will find these and other items of interest in the *Free Resources* area.

1. Top Ten Worst Hiring Mistakes (Chapter 5)
2. Success Factor Worksheet (Chapter 6)
3. Samples of Success Factors (Chapter 6)
4. Sourcing Case Studies (Chapter 7)
5. Examples of Compelling Marketing Statements (Chapter 7)
6. Thirty-Minute Success Factor Phone Screen (Chapter 9)
7. Templates for each of the Five Key Questions (Chapter 10)
8. Homework Assignments (Chapter 10)
9. Eight-Dimension Success Matrix Form (Chapter 11)
10. Eight-Point Success Validation Form (Chapter 11)

Appendix 3: The Study

The Top Ten Hiring Mistakes CEOs Make: Case-Based Analysis
And Recommendations

ABSTRACT

An after-action review study combining the analysis of 225 executive searches in 134 companies studied, interviews with hiring executives, and a review of secondary research.

Problem Statement

Best practices for executive hiring in a wide range of industries have yet to be clearly defined and implemented. There is substantial debate and disagreement about the best approaches, as well as an imprecise understanding of the root causes of high-level executive failure soon after hire (18 months to two years).

Relevance Of The Topic

The amount of time, money, and organizational performance repercussions at stake in high-level executive hiring is enormous. Published rates of new executive failure (defined narrowly to cover a new hire who leaves the position voluntarily or involuntarily within two years of initial hire) range from a conservative 30% to as high as 40%. Supplementing the published failure rates with our own proprietary survey of more than 20,000 hiring executives conducted over the past 15 years, the failure rate reaches a staggering 56% when the definition of "failure" is expanded to include "Significantly under-performing when compared with company expectations."

With high-stakes competition for top talent at an all-time high and a lack of replicable hiring methods to improve outcomes, CEOs and hiring executives need a reliable framework for identifying, sourcing, selecting, and transitioning the best prospects for success.

Data Collection Techniques

Two steps were used to collect data: secondary research and case study analysis primary research (survey).

- A first step was an analysis of secondary research studies.
- The second step was an examination of 225 case studies within 134 hiring companies spanning two decades to better understand the common hiring practices that are positively correlated with high rates of new executive failure.

Secondary Data Analysis

Among the highlights of articles and publications we surveyed to help direct our research, highlights of findings included:

- Clearly stating and prioritizing expectations from the start reduces the rate of failure. (Andersson, 1999)
- Companies that are unwilling to consider ramifications of a switch for the job candidate are less likely to be successful at the offer stage. (*Executive Search Review*, 2003)
- Eleven behavioral indicators correlate strongly with executive failure. These are: Arrogance, Melodrama, Volatility, Excessive Caution, Habitual Distrust, Aloofness, Mischievousness, Eccentricity, Passive Resistance, Perfectionism, and Eagerness to Please. (Cairo and Dotlich, 2003)
- 70% of executive failures are due to bad execution of strategies. A major part of this is their inability to put the right people into the right jobs and the related issue of not fixing people problems quickly. (Charan and Colvin, 1999)
- Many managers who are put on the track to become the next CEO never make it due to their focus on the wrong issues. Several necessary capabilities, such as managing the political environment and personal style, separate the merely good CEO candidate from the elite one that will actually make it to the top spot. (Ciampa, 2005)

- Failure to treat potential candidates with respect is among the top "fatal mistakes" that can lead to the demise of an entire company by starving the organization of talent. (Corcodillos)
- Failure to adapt to new circumstances, or "business school logic gone bad," is a recurrent and common theme in executive failure. (Finkelstein, 2003)
- In one industry (construction), fully 65% of CEOs who were promoted internally failed to meet owner's expectations for growth and lose market share. This indicates that industry knowledge and experience, along with intimate knowledge of a company's inner workings and culture, are not as important as other skills in a leadership position. (Hornberger Management Company, 2003)
- Examining how the candidate solved problems in the past will help reveal how they will solve them in the future; concurrently, if a candidate is not deeply challenged in the interview process, the company could pay a price. (Joiner, 2004)
- Assimilation coaching within the first 100 days helps to reduce rates of executive failure. Some incoming executives hire coaches themselves, recognizing the need for additional support during transition. (Lewis, 2003)
- The rate of CEO turnover due to poor performance is rapidly accelerating (increased by 130 percent between 1995 and 2001, and closer to 300 percent in 2002). (Lucier *et. al.*, 2003)
- In most new executive hires, integration takes longer than anticipated. 51% of those surveyed felt that integration takes longer than they expect, since though most hoped it would take 6 months, the reality was between 9 and 18 months. (RHR International, 2002)
- The development of clear criteria for executive selection is too often pushed aside in the face of more immediate challenges. (Sessa and Taylor, 2000)

These data and additional hypotheses drawn from preliminary interviews with hiring executives were amalgamated to form a taxonomic "hiring mistakes" grid, which was applied diagnostically to 225 search cases in 134 companies.

Primary Data Analysis

The hiring practices in place at the hiring company at the time of two-hundred twenty-five executive hires in 134 target companies were diagnosed. Of the organizations analyzed, 46.2% were manufacturing companies; 14.9% were in the high technology sector; 16.4% represented distribution concerns; and 22.4% were retail or service industry companies. No significant differences were found among the individual sectors, so data were combined for the purposes of analysis.

The following table summarizes the frequency and rank of the top ten most frequent mistakes. It was not uncommon for difficult searches to manifest several of the mistakes at the same time. In addition, the survey covered only hiring practices in place *before* the targeted companies revamped them through an executive search engagement. As such, these data represent a "control" baseline, most likely representative of organizations that have never undertaken a structured re-deployment in their hiring practices.

Hiring Mistake	# Of Searches	% Of Searches	Mistake Rank By Frequency
Inadequate job descriptions drove the hiring process; focused solely on experience and skills (not company expectations).	209	93	1
Superficial interviewing: Did not put candidates under magnifying glass, verify claims, and check facts.	207	92	2
Inappropriate "Prerequisites" Used Too Early In Selection Process: Over-emphasis on specific education, technical skills, and industry experience screened out qualified candidates.	171	76	3

Snap Judgment: Hiring teams relied too heavily on first impressions to make final hiring decisions.	162	72	4
Historical Bias: Using only past performance to predict future results.	153	68	5
Performance Bias: Failure to understand interview and job performance are two different things; making an offer to the "best actor," not the best candidate.	142	63	6
Fishing in shallow waters: Structuring the search to attract only the bottom third Aggressive candidates; not actively seeking out Selective and Sleeper candidates.	128	57	7

Failure To Probe For Core Success Factors: Not looking for evidence of the five best predictors of long-term success (self-motivation, leadership, comparable past performance, job-specific problem solving, adaptability).	126	56	8
Ignoring Top Candidate's Needs: Not understanding what motivates top talent to take a job.	124	55	9
Desperation Hiring: Not budgeting enough time for the search, resulting in shallow sourcing and superficial interviews.	123	55	10

In our experience, the hiring mistakes identified in this survey are not caused by willful ignorance or negligence. Most often, hires that do not produce the results desired are the result of a predictable combination of causal factors.

- **Inadequate preparation.** Rarely had the company outlined a detailed, measurable definition of "success" that could be used to source, evaluate, and select candidates. Instead, most hiring organizations relied on outdated or insufficient job specs that merely listed desired attributes, educational attainment, and so on.
- **Lack of information.** After our work with the surveyed

companies, nearly all dramatically improved hiring practices and (most importantly) the performance of new hires. We conclude, therefore, that at least one cause of their former hiring failures was not endemic organizational dysfunction, but a lack of information and training about how to hire more effectively at the executive level.

- **"Human nature."** Interpersonal situations like interviews, conducted in a vacuum, are often guided primarily by gut feelings. The hiring team who has not been trained to minimize these distractions are easily influenced by preconscious perceptions and nonverbal cues. When provided with a tool set designed to counterbalance these biases, the interview team performance is far more likely to overcome distractions and focus on more critical, success-based matters.

Other Considerations

Additional pitfalls in hiring practices were also identified throughout the process of completing the analysis. While these occurred less often than the top ten mistakes, these missteps and errors manifested frequently enough to warrant mention. Readers who are assessing their own organization's hiring practices would do well to also examine their procedures to root out the following.

- Ignoring cultural mismatches when hiring
- Not physically preparing (reception, waiting area, greeting, etc.) for successful interviews
- Failure to create compelling marketing campaigns to attract top talent to open positions
- Passive sourcing (waiting for resumes to come in rather than actively pursuing Sleeper and Selective candidates)
- Lack of preparation for interviews; no written questions
- Failure to evaluate candidates against an objective definition of success

Conclusions

With the most common hiring mistakes in mind, and based on two decades of hands-on experience helping Fortune 1000 organizations improve sustainable and successful hiring practices, we created the Success Factor Methodology™. This structured approach to executive hiring helps our client companies avoid repeating predictable, avoidable hiring pitfalls that plague many high-level hires.

This methodology comprises eight separate steps that require significant up-front strategic consideration, gap analysis, and process preparation. The outcome is a hire that with a significantly increased likelihood of long-term success.

The eight steps are:

1. Build a multi-faceted Success Factor Snapshot™ to guide the entire search process
2. Implement a deep sourcing strategy to reach and attract Selective and Sleeper Candidates
3. Identify and verify success prospects
4. Create structured profiles on selected candidates to enable objective, unbiased evaluation, and comparison
5. Conduct Success-Factor-based interviews using five key questions
6. Proactively address and overcome obstacles to hire throughout the entire active interviewing process
7. Facilitate compensation and benefit negotiations through interview-based groundwork early in the process
8. Facilitate assimilation coaching to ensure the executive is successful from the first day

Each step in the Success Factor Methodology requires full collaboration across stakeholders in business units affected by the upcoming hire.

Implications For Further Research

Opportunities for follow-up research to this initial diagnostic study could involve

- Tracking changes in new hire success and failure rates at companies that adopt and integrate the Success Factor Methodology approach to hiring
- Testing the persistence and longevity of new behaviors, with and without periodic reinforcement and retraining in the Success Factor Methodology
- An analysis of applicant quality and quantity using Success Factor Methodology "compelling marketing" sourcing techniques vs. traditional methods
- A qualitative, interview-based assessment of candidate perceptions of the Success Factor Methodology hiring methodology from the "other side"

Recommendations

Organizations must learn from the mistakes of others and revise hiring and selection practices to circumvent the most predictable and preventable mistakes in executive hiring. We recommend a comprehensive, collaborative strategy involving all stakeholders within a hiring organization, including HR, the executive suite, and departments that will be directly impacted by an executive hire. All involved parties must be briefed and trained on common pitfalls and provided with specific toolsets to help offset and minimize the effects of longstanding habit on the hiring process.

Works Consulted

"Recruiters Face More Obstacles in Convincing Candidates to Move." *Executive Search Review* Sept. 2003

"Understanding Failure." *Across The Board* July/Aug. 2003: 27.

Andersson, Don. "Avoid Executive Failure Traps." *Executive Excellence*

July 1999: 16.

Association of Executive Search Consultants. "Executive Resume Poll." April 2004 <http://www.aesc.org>.

Association of Executive Search Consultants. "Underutilized Executive Skills Poll." March 2004 <http://www.aesc.org>.

Boren, Susan S., and Heidrick, Robert L. "Get serious to make CEO evaluations work." *Spencer Stuart Governance Letter* 2004: 54-56. <http://www.spencerstuart.com>.

Cairo, Peter C., and Dotlich, David L. *Why CEOs Fail: The 11 Behaviors That Can Derail Your Climb to the Top and How to Manage Them.* Indianapolis: Jossey-Bass, 2003.

Center for Advanced Human Resource Studies. "Waging the War for Talent." *HR Spectrum* Sept.-Oct. 1999: 1, 4, 6.

Charan, Ram. "Ending the CEO Succession Crisis." *Harvard Business Review* Feb. 2005: 72.

Charan, Ram and Colvin, Geoffery. "Why CEOs Fail" *Fortune* 21 June 1999: 68.

Christian & Timbers. "Trends in Executive Suite: COOs Train and Transition for the CEO Position." 2004 <http://www.ctnet. com>.

Ciampa, Dan. "Almost Ready: How Leaders Move Up." *Harvard Business Review* Jan. 2005: 46.

Citrin, James M., and Neff, Thomas J. "Now You're In Charge: The First 100 Days." *Chief Executive Officer* 2003.

Corcodilos, Nick. "Death By Lethal Reputation: The Demise of An Employer." <http://www.asktheheadhunter.com>.

Daurn, Julie. "Corporate Governance and Director Selection: A new role for human resource executives." Originally published in *Restoring Trust: HR's Role in Corporate Governance.* Human Resource Planning Society, 2003. <http://www.spencerstuart.com>.

Deal, Jennifer J., Sessa, Valerie I., and Taylor, Jodi J. "Choosing Executives: A Research Report on Peak Selection Simulation." Center for Creative Leadership Press, 1999.

Finkelstein, Sydney. *Why Smart Executives Fail: And What You Can Learn From Their Mistakes.* Portfolio, 2003.

Global Consulting Partnership. "Executive Coaching: An Investment In Creating Masterful Leadership." *Executive Coaching* 2000.

Global Consulting Partnership. "Executive Development and Succession Planning." 2000 <http://www.tgcpinc.com/tgcp.html>.

Grossman, Robert J. "Forging a Partnership—Executive Turnover." *HR Magazine* April 2003.

Hornberger Management Company. "Construction Executive Retention Survey." 2003 <http://www.hmc.com>.

Joiner, Harry. "How To Identify A Problem Solver." *6 Figure Jobs.com E-Newsletter* Sept. 2004. <http://www.6figurejobs.com>.

Lewis, Diane. "Top Firms Enlisting Coaches For New Execs Practice Intended to Smooth Transition, Increase Retention." *The Boston Globe* 9 Mar. 2003: G1.

Lucier, Chuck, Schuyt, Rob and Spiegel, Eric. "Why CEOs Fall–The Causes and Consequences of Turnover at the Top." *Booz Allen Hamilton Special Report* May 2003.

Mendels, Pamela. "Gone But Not Forgotten." *Business Week* June 2001.

Paese, Matthew J. "Growing Your Own Leaders: The 'Acceleration' Center." *Development Dimensions International* <http://www.ddiworld.com>.

Parker, Brian. "Construction Executive Hiring Permanently Changes After War." *Construction Executive A/E/C Newswire* 15 Apr. 2003 <http://www.constructionexecutive.com>.

Rafter, Michelle V. "Candidates for jobs in high places sit for tests that size up their mettle." *Workforce Management* May 2004: 70.

Recruiters Network. "Creating the Perfect Candidate Interviewing Experience From Concept to Reality." *6 Figure Jobs.com E-Newsletter* July 2004. <http://www.6figurejobs.com>.

RHR International. "Hitting the Ground Running: Accelerating Executive Integration." *Executive Research* Sept. 2002. <http://www.rhrinternational.com>.

Rock, Michael E. "Avoiding Costly Hiring Mistakes." *Six Figure Jobs.com E-Newsletter* Jan. 2003. <http://www.6figurejobs.com>.

Rubin, Debra K. "Executive Recruiters Are More Than Boardroom Brokers." *Engineering News-Record* 22 Dec. 2003: 22.

Sessa, Valerie I., and Taylor, Jodi J. *Executive Selection: Strategies for Success.* Indianapolis: Jossey-Bass Publishers, 2000.

Strauss, Gary. "Troubled Firms Entice CEOs With Platinum Pay." *USA Today* 21 Feb. 2003: 1B.

Watkins, Michael. *The First 90 Days: Critical Success Strategies For New Leaders At All Levels.* Cambridge: Harvard Business School Press, 2003.

About The Authors

IMPACT Hiring Solutions is a nationally recognized retained executive search firm. In addition to its search practice, through its in-house workshops and seminars, IHS helps companies reduce turnover, retain top talent and become talent magnets. The firm's partners have assisted and coached thousands of CEOs, key executives, managers and other executive recruiters to increase hiring accuracy and build high performing teams through their proprietary Success Factor Methodology™.

Janet Boydell has interviewed thousands of candidates for managerial and executive positions during the past twelve years. Her expertise includes searches for small to mid-sized companies for positions in finance, operations, human resources, sales and marketing across such industries as manufacturing and technology.

In addition to retained search, Janet presents in-house training seminars that teach hiring teams how to break old habits, learn effective interviewing techniques, and implement proven hiring practices that significantly increase hiring accuracy.

Prior to IMPACT Hiring Solutions, Janet's professional background included 10 years as a Vice President with CJA Executive Search.

Previously, Janet held a Series 27 Financial and Operations Principal license from the NASD and worked for investment banking organizations such as MOKG, Wedbush Morgan Securities and Cantor Fitzgerald. Janet earned her Bachelor of Science in Business Administration from California State Polytechnic University, Pomona.

Barry Deutsch is a well-known thought leader in hiring and peak performance management. He is a frequent and sought-after speaker for management meetings, trade associations, and CEO forums such as The Executive Committee (TEC) and Young President's Organization (YPO). Many of his clients view him as their virtual "Chief Talent Officer."

Barry brings to the table a vast knowledge base of twenty years in the executive search field, with a track record of successful placements in such diverse environments as multi-billion dollar Fortune 100 companies, entrepreneurial firms, and middle-market high-growth businesses. He has worked closely with thousands of CEOs and Key Executives to help improve hiring success, leverage human capital, and raise the bar on talent acquisition.

Barry earned his BA and MA from American University in Washington, DC. Prior to his executive search career, Barry held positions of responsibility in Finance and General Management with Mattel, Beatrice Foods, and Westinghouse Cable.

Brad Remillard, an executive recruiter for more than twenty years, has conducted over 4,000 interviews and has been directly involved in over 1,000 executive searches. A CPA and graduate of California State University, Fullerton, Brad previously served as President of CJA Executive Search, which was recognized as one of the top retained search firms in Southern California. Brad has conducted nationwide searches ranging from Fortune 500 executive vacancies to small, entrepreneurial companies. His search expertise includes General Management (CEO, COO GM), Sales and Marketing, Manufacturing and Operations, Accounting, Finance, Human Resources, and Information Systems.

In 1999 Brad co-founded the American Association of Senior Executives (AASE), one of Southern California 's largest career management and business resource organizations exclusively dedicated to VP and C-level executives. The AASE has assisted more the 1,500 corporate executives manage their careers. Brad has personally coached many of these executives on success-based interviewing, 21st century networking techniques, and career transition. He is a frequent speaker on the subject of career management and executive networking.

Printed in the United States
82239LV00007B/18